The Reality, Mythology, and Fantasies Of Unicorns

by
W. B. J. Williams

Dragonwell Publishing

W. B. J. Williams

The Reality, Mythology, and Fantasies of Unicorns

Copyright © 2021 by W. B. J. Williams

Published by Dragonwell Publishing
www.dragonwellpublishing.com

ISBN 978-1-940076-56-0

All rights reserved.
No part of this book may be reproduced or transmitted in any printed or electronic form without permission in writing from the publisher, nor be otherwise circulated in any form other than that in which it is published.

TABLE OF CONTENTS

Foreword	1
The Unicorn as Found in History and Archaeology	5
The Myth of the Endless Battle Between the Lion and the Unicorn	35
The Myth of the Unicorn Hunt	59
The Mythology of the Unicorn's Horn	71
The Unicorn in Art and Literature	79
Making Unicorns	103
Image credits	108
Bibliography	113
About the Author	120

By the same author:

THE GARDEN AT THE ROOF OF THE WORLD

FOREWORD

Have you ever hunted for a unicorn? I have. When my eldest daughter was about seven, she had tired of the many books appropriate for her age and started asking me to tell her new stories. Figuring that she might enjoy a story about a young woman with a unicorn, I started to create such a tale. During the telling and retelling, I became convinced I had the bones of a good novel.

I started to do some research on unicorns, as there is something about me that wants to place a story in an appropriate context. I wanted a believable backstory, a milieu in which a unicorn would belong, and as thorough an understanding of the subject matter as possible. As unicorns come from our history and our mythological past, I would set my story in the historical past. I took a lot of notes, some of which made it into the appendix of the novel. My hunt for a unicorn was on.

I made the choice to set *The Garden at the Roof of the World* in the mid-thirteenth century CE. I also decided to treat all the mythology of the era as if it were true, not just that unicorns were real. To me this was an essential step.

To my way of thinking, you can't depict a time and a place unless you get the attitudes and beliefs of the people who lived in that century correct. As so many of the attitudes and beliefs of that era are very different from my own, and from what

The Reality, Mythology, and Fantasies of Unicorns

is acceptable in our modern era, this was often difficult. Some folks would argue that since I was writing a fantasy, I could just make it all up. You must have read many historical fantasies where you find modern people in a historical setting. However, I must maintain that a historical fantasy must be as faithful as possible to what was, and so I did a lot of research.

Like the myth of the dragon, the myth of the unicorn is found across many of the cultures of our world, with legends that are remarkable in their consistency. Unicorns are beasts. Unicorns are sacred. They are dangerous. There is a curious link between unicorns and virgins, between unicorns and lions. Unicorns are solitary creatures, avoiding all others.

The middle of the thirteenth century is one of those rare times in history when new ideas flourished and grew, and people shared discoveries across great distances. If it hadn't been for the Black Death a century later, what we know to be the Renaissance period might have started earlier.

In the thirteenth century, the Silk Road was still open to Europeans. It was soon to be closed by the Ottoman Turks, which would cause the Europeans to seek a way to China and India by sea. Both the Roman (Byzantine) Empire and the Caliphate were still in existence in the mid-thirteenth century. The Caliphate would not survive the end of the century, destroyed by the same Mongols that had overrun much of Eastern Europe. The Principality of Antioch would also collapse before the end of the thirteenth century as would the Seljuk Sultanate. The Chola Empire of South India would not outlive the century, but the Delhi Sultanate had yet to conquer the principal fortifications in west Rajasthan where the Jain tradition had flourished. The world of the fourteenth century would be very different than the world that came before it. Much of the ancient world perished during the thirteenth century.

In the thirteenth century, we have the account of Marco Polo traveling along the Silk Road and encountering a unicorn on his return trip through India. In setting my story in the thirteenth century, I not only chose a time when people still believed in unicorns, I set the story in a time when perhaps people still encountered unicorns in their travels.

The events of the novel occur in the thirteenth century, at a time before the Black Death left Christianity with only those priests too cowardly to minister to the sick. People could still travel across all of Europe and Asia following trade and pilgrimage routes that would soon be closed. Women were openly contributing to art, music, and literature. Those who think deeply and richly—not just the philosophers, but theologians, poets, musicians, and artists—were sharing ideas across cultures and religions, and being praised, not censured, for their efforts. It was a time when, if you believe contemporary authors, the last of the unicorns still lived. It was certainly a time when the myth of the unicorn was widely celebrated.

I wish to share with you what I learned of that rarest of creatures, the unicorn. I already mentioned that I took a lot of notes, and this volume has its origins in those notes. I have organized this book as follows: first I will explore what we can find in both the historical and archaeological record regarding unicorns and their role in human history. Secondly, I'll look at myth of the endless battle between the lion and the unicorn. I'll explore the myth of the unicorn hunt next, followed by the myths associated over the centuries with the horn itself. I'll spend some time looking at how the unicorn has been portrayed in art and literature. I'll then briefly look at how people have been manipulating the horns of sheep and bulls to make unicorns, and how that contrasts with other horn manipulation in pastoral cultures globally.

While my book is about a subject that many consider to be at once fictional and mythological, the unicorn known to us scientifically as Elasmotherium was real, once upon a time as it were. They went extinct a long time ago. Because of this, and like many of those who have written about the unicorn before me, I've approached the subject as I would any non-fiction. Multiple Ph.D. dissertations could come from the source material, and I encourage and applaud anyone who takes this up and goes further than I could.

As with all scholars who have an interest in the unicorn, I am heavily indebted to Odell Shepard. However, the translations available to me benefit from a hundred years of additional scholarship than those available to him, so I have sought out more contemporary translations of the same sources where possible. I must note that Odell Shepard has a discernible bias against certain of his sources, and he often scorns the material he examines. You can read Odell Shepard's book for free on Sacred-Texts.org. If you are a student of the unicorn, I highly recommend reading his work. Robert Brown's manuscript is also available for free on Sacred-Texts.org. His manuscript provided me much of my understanding of the unicorn in heraldic art. His theories on how this ties into a larger mythological context are interesting and worth pursuing based upon the evidence he presents. I also owe much to the work of Rüdiger Robert Beer, whose *Unicorn: Myth and Reality* has a wealth of images and subtle details regarding the mythology of the beast. I am deeply in the debt of the doctoral research of Dr. Hall on the "Assyrian Moon God" and of Dr. Giovino on *The Assyrian Sacred Tree*. Chris Lavers picks up where Odell Shepard leaves off and provides excellent information on those who have hunted in vain for a unicorn, as well as how pastoralists have been creating unicorns for centuries. There are many fun texts written about the unicorn for all ages. My favorite is Paul and Karin Johnsgard's *A Natural History of Dragons and Unicorns*, with Juliette Wood's *Fantastic Creatures in Mythology and Folklore* as a close second. I don't reference these in my own writing, but I did enjoy reading them. You will find a complete bibliography at the end of the text for those who want to take things further.

May you be so fortunate as to one day see a wild unicorn in your garden. If you do, follow it where it leads.

THE UNICORN AS FOUND IN HISTORY AND ARCHAEOLOGY

In contemporary times we've come to expect that a unicorn will have a rainbow tail and be the toy of choice for a very young child. Yet you have to look no further than the roof of the Old State House in Boston to see that once upon a time, or just a few hundred years ago, unicorns were the perfect symbol of royalty. To the European medieval imagination, the unicorn was both a real and ferocious beast to be found and tamed only by a virginal maiden, as well as a mystical symbol of Christian mythology. In medieval Asia, you'll again find the unicorn untamable, a mighty validation of power and a messenger of the gods.

Only the dragon has captured the imaginations of peoples across the globe like the unicorn, and the unicorn is the only mythological creature that people were still seeking in the nineteenth century CE. While some would explain away the myth using the rhinoceros, they forget that most kinds of rhinoceros have more than one horn, and even when there is just one horn, it is set on the edge of the nose, not on the forehead. All tales of the unicorn place the horn on the top of the head, like the horns of a goat or bull.

Only a Hollywood movie makes the unicorn look like a horse. Some myths compare them to an ass, large and fierce. Others compare the unicorn to a goat. The horn isn't always white, it is often golden, green, multihued, or black. The horn is thought to heal with a touch, to cure poisons if ingested, or to purify water. Thus, many a sailor got rich selling a narwhal tooth to a gullible aristocrat. Queen Elizabeth I of England was duped into paying a fortune for a beautiful but quite unmagical narwhal tooth.

Looking at the archaeological record, unicorns are probably based on the memory of elasmotherium, a rather large relative of the rhinoceros which had a single horn that grew from its forehead. Recent findings suggest that the creature survived into the agricultural era, though was possibly extinct well in advance of written history. The most recent specimens found in the western Siberian plain are from about thirty-five thousand years ago, but there is cave art in France that depicts the beast which dates to perhaps as recent as 15,000 years ago. This is about the time of the end of the last ice age and the extinction of the mammoth. Humanity began to develop pastoral and agriculture economies, as well as the domestication of animals during this era.

Elasmotherium was about the size of a mammoth, being over six feet tall, over fifteen feet in length, and weighing over three tons. Unlike its cousin, the rhinoceros, the elasmotherium's horn sat on the forehead, squarely between the eyes. Many of the ancient descriptions of the unicorn match the reconstructions, though we have no evidence if the colors recorded by any particular observer are correct.

Like all rhinos, elasmotheres were herbivorous. Evidence suggests that their high crowned molars were ever-growing, much like the front teeth of a rodent. This means that elasmotheres needed to be constantly chewing, which was likely in any event due to the nature of their diet. First discovered in 1809, the name comes from the Ancient Greek, elasmos, which means laminated—inspired by the folding of the teeth. DNA extracted from surviving tissue shows that elasmotherium diverged from the main line of rhinoceros about 47.8 million years ago. Its legs, much longer than those of its surviving relatives, were adapted for galloping, much like a modern horse.

The drawing in Figure 1 is a duplication of the first published sketch of what we believe the beast must have looked like, drawn by Rashevsky in 1878. However, this is not the oldest artwork depicting elasmotherium.

Figure 1. The first published sketch of Elasmotherium, drawn by Rashevsky in 1878

Among the many works of paleolithic art found in the Rouffignac cave in France there is believed to be a rendering of an elasmotherium made by those who saw the beast. This tantalizing yet incomplete sketch is probably the only picture we have of a unicorn drawn by people who actually saw the animal in the wild, and not in their imaginations.

The art found in the cave has not been directly dated except by stylistic comparison with art found in other caves which have been dated. This method shows that the art was likely drawn roughly from 13,000 to 15,000 years ago.

Humans of this period in this part of France were anatomically modern *Homo sapiens sapiens*, though short of stature, with lower-than-average foreheads and prominent brow ridges. They often lived in tents, and seem to have been migratory, following both the herds they hunted and the life cycle of the flora they ate. Their tools were made of bone, antler, ivory,

The Reality, Mythology, and Fantasies of Unicorns

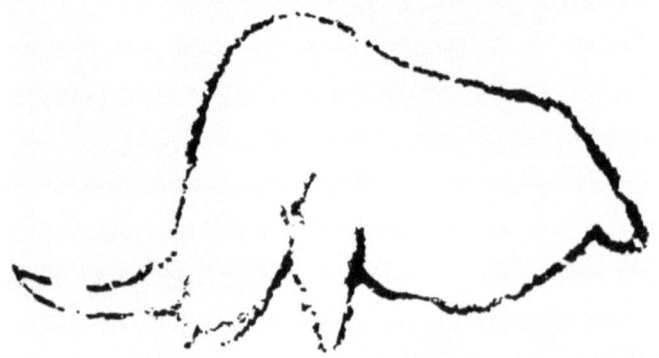

Figure 2. Paleolithic art from the Rouffignac cave in France, believed to depict an elasmotherium

as well as stone. One period drawing of a person being bitten by a snake shows the person naked, which speaks to the climate being warm at least part of the year, despite the presence of reindeer, mammoth, and of course, elasmotherium.

The beast is typically reconstructed as a wooly animal, with fur similar to that of a mammoth. It is known to have had only three toes, much like modern rhinos. Their horns are thought to be keratinous, indicated by a circular dome on the forehead with a 13-centimeter-deep furrowed surface and a circumference of 0.9 meters. The furrows are interpreted as seats of blood vessels for horn-generating tissues, much like what is found in modern horn-growing rhinos. Modern rhinos don't grow their horns from the bone, but from the surface of a dense skin tissue anchored through bone irregularities.

The teeth and the orientation of the head suggest that elasmotherium had a diet similar to that of the white rhino. The head of the elasmotherium had the most obtuse angle of any of the rhinos, giving it easy access to the lowest-growing plants. The timing of the last known archaeological discoveries shows that elasmotherium likely disappeared during the larger Pleistocene extinction, along with every animal species over 45 kg in that part of Siberia (*Kosintse et al. 31–38*). This period of history also saw the introduction of modern humans into the area.

Fossil evidence suggests that the elasmotherium species had a range that spanned from the location of the present-day Moldova to the east, through the steppes of east Asia. However, while we have not found any fossils in western Europe, the painting found in the French cave suggests either that elasmotherium had a wider range than currently understood from the archaeology, or that the drawing was made by someone to illustrate the beast to people who had never seen one (*Schvyreva, 128*).

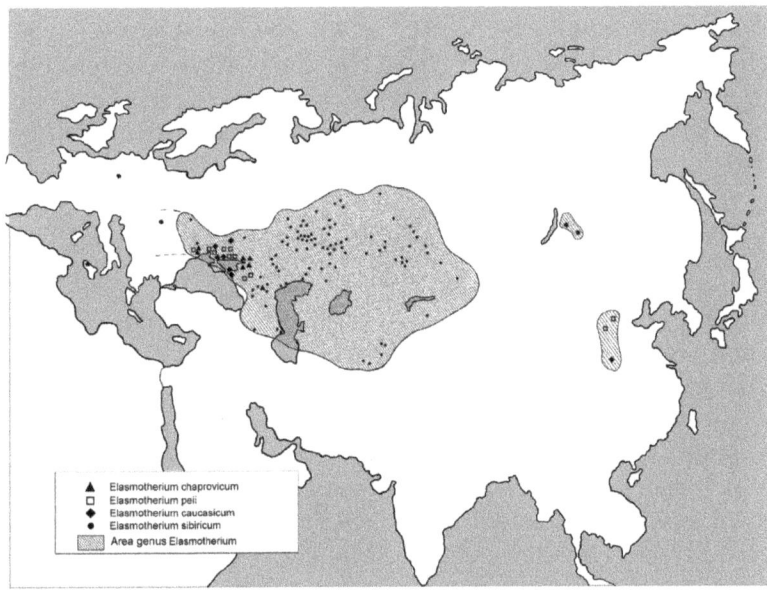

Figure 3 (Schvyreva, 130). The map of Eurasia during the Pleistocene, showing the areas inhabited by different elasmotherium species, as suggested by fossil evidence.

It is important to note as we move from archaeology to history that I will often make references to mythology, which we'll explore in detail in later chapters. Until recently, historians and scholars did not separate mythology from any other area of knowledge. In most places in the world, you still find a frequent mingling of mythology with how history is understood. Unlike some of my sources on the subject of unicorns, I don't find this a frustrating reality. Humans weave stories, beliefs, history, and science together with elegance, amusement, and often with profound results. This is part of what it means to be human. That the unicorn both existed as a historical animal and as a mythological being is an excellent example of how humanity looks to transcend our knowledge of how the universe works. Sometimes our mythology produces dangerous results, such as the belief that the horn of a unicorn can cure poison. Attempts to apply this principle in practice would end in disaster. At other times, it is our scientific exploration that produces dangerous results, such as genetically engineered pathogens and nuclear fission, to name a few. It is our stories that help us understand both and teach us how to avoid the nightmares that happen when either myth or science is followed uncritically.

What is interesting is how often the description in a historical record could imply that the author was describing an elasmotherium. One of the earliest and certainly more influential western descriptions of a unicorn comes from Ctesias of Cnidus, a Greek physician who lived in the fifth century BCE. Only fragments of his work, *Indica*, survived to the present day. The translation of an excerpt of *Indica* found in the work of the Byzantine scholar Photius says:

> "In India there are wild asses as large as horses, or even larger. Their body is white, their head dark red, their eyes bluish, and they have a horn in their forehead about a cubit in length. The lower part of the horn, for about two palms distance from the forehead, is quite white, the middle is black, the upper part, which terminates in a point, is a very flaming red. Those who drink out of cups made from it are proof against convulsions, epilepsy, and even poison, provided that before or after having taken it they drink some wine or water or other liquid out of these cups. The domestic and wild asses of other countries and all other solid-hoofed animals have neither huckle-bones nor gallbladder, whereas the Indian asses have both. Their huckle-bone is the most beautiful that I have seen, like that of the ox in size and appearance; it is as heavy as lead and of the color of cinnabar all through. These animals are very strong and swift; neither the horse nor any other animal can overtake them. At first they run slowly, but the longer they run their pace increases wonderfully, and becomes faster and faster. There is only one way of catching them. When they take their young to feed, if they are surrounded by a large number of horsemen, being unwilling to abandon their foals, they show fight, butt with their horns, kick, bite, and kill many men and horses. They are at last taken, after they have been pierced with arrows and spears; for it is impossible to capture them alive. Their flesh is too bitter to eat, and they are only hunted for the sake of the horns and huckle-bones." (*Photius*)

The dimensions for the horn roughly match modern estimates of the elasmotherium's horn, not the horn of a known modern rhino. No known modern rhino has the coloring that

Ctesias described, but we don't have any soft tissue samples to help identify the coloring of the elasmotherium.

None other than Aristotle believed Ctesias' account, and further wrote on the subject in his *History of Animals* of the appearance of the unicorn:

> "The great majority of the horned animals are cloven-footed, as the ox, the stag, the goat; and a solid-hooved animal with a pair of horns has never yet been met with. But a few animals are known to be single-horned and single-hooved, as the Indian ass; and one, to wit the oryx, is single-horned and cloven-hooved." (*Aristotle, Book 2, Part 1*)

> "Of all solid-hooved animals the Indian ass alone has an astragalus or huckle-bone; for the pig, as was said above, is either solid-hooved or cloven-footed, and consequently has no well-formed huckle-bone. Of the cloven footed many are provided with a huckle-bone." (*Aristotle, Book 2, Part 1*)

The huckle-bone, or talus, is the large bone in the ankle that articulates with the tibia and the calcaneum and navicular bone of the foot.

It is partially because of that ankle bone that many modern scholars have wondered if the description that Ctesias gives is a remarkably inaccurate account of the one horned Indian rhino, which still lives in the river valleys of northern India. Certainly, the description of how the beast, when it runs, starts slowly and builds up speed as it goes matches the description of how a modern Indian rhino runs. However, nothing else in the description matches, not the coloration of the skin and fur, not the colors of the horn, nor the size of the horn match. It would make more sense that he was describing a different animal that also had a solid hoof with a huckle-bone, such as elasmotherium.

Pliny the Elder wrote in his *Natural History*:

> "There are in India oxen also with solid hoofs and a single horn; and a wild beast called the axis, which has a skin like that of a fawn, but with numerous spots on it, and whiter; this animal is looked upon as sacred to Bacchus. The Orsæan Indians hunt down a kind of ape, which has the body white all over; as well as a very fierce animal called the monoceros, which has the head of the stag, the feet of the elephant, and the tail of the boar, while the rest of the body is like that of the horse;

it makes a deep lowing noise, and has a single black horn, which projects from the middle of its forehead, two cubits in length. This animal, it is said, cannot be taken alive." (*Pliny the Elder, Book 8, Chapter 31*)

Obviously, the elder Pliny was not writing from direct observation, as he never went to India, and so his description calls upon simile to help his readers understand what the beast must look like.

Glaudius Aelianus in his *On Animals* wrote:

"I have learned that in India are born wild asses as big as horses. All their body is white except for the head, which approaches purple, while their eyes give off a dark blue color. They have a horn on their forehead as much as a cubit and a half long; the lower part of the horn is white, the upper part is crimson, while the middle is jet-black. From these variegated horns, I am told, the Indians drink, but not all, only the most eminent Indians, and round them at intervals they lay rings of gold, as though they were decorating the beautiful arm of a statue with bracelets. And they say that a man who has drunk from this horn knows not, and is free from, incurable diseases: he will never be seized with convulsions nor with the sacred sickness, as it is called, nor be destroyed by poisons. Moreover, if he has previously drunk some deadly stuff, he vomits it up and is restored to health.

It is believed that asses, both the tame and the wild kind, all the world over and all other beasts with uncloven hoofs are without knucklebones and without gall in the liver; whereas those horned asses of India, Ctesias says, have knucklebones and are not without gall. Their knucklebones are said to be black, and if ground down are black inside as well. And these animals are far swifter than any ass or even than any horse or any deer. They begin to run, it is true, at a gentle pace, but gradually gather strength until to pursue them is, in the language of poetry, to chase the unattainable.

When the mother gives birth and leads her new-born colts about, the fathers herd with, and look after, them. And these asses frequent the most desolate plains in India. So, when the Indians go to hunt them, the asses allow their colts, still tender and young, to pasture in their rear, while they themselves fight on their behalf and join battle with the horsemen and strike them with their horns. Now the strength of these horns is such that nothing can withstand their blows, but everything gives way and snaps or, it may be, is shattered and rendered useless. They have in the past even struck at the ribs of a horse, ripped it open, and disemboweled it. For that reason, the horsemen dread coming to close quarters with them, since the penalty for so doing is a most lamentable death, and both they and their horses are killed. They can kick fearfully too. Moreover, their bite goes so deep that they tear away everything that they have grasped. A full-grown ass one would never capture alive: they are shot with javelins and arrows, and when dead the Indians strip them of their horns, which, as I said, they decorate.

But the flesh of Indian asses is uneatable, the reason being that it is naturally exceedingly bitter." (*Aelian, Book 4, Paragraph 52*)

It is important to note that the behavior he describes is rather typical of the rhinoceros, but this doesn't mean that it wouldn't have been observed in the larger cousin of the rhinoceros, the elasmotherium, had they survived this late in history. Despite this being an accurate description of the behavior of the rhino, no known rhino ever had a horn on its forehead, except for the four species of elasmotherium. It is not likely that the behavior could be so accurately described and the location of the horn so badly mistaken. Possible, but not likely.

I want to take careful note of one other item in Glaudius Aelianus's description, that people drank from the horn in the belief that doing so cured them of diseases and made them proof to poisons. The horns of modern rhinos are hollow, and it is to be expected that elasmotherium horns would also be hollow, making them rather large drinking vessels. This supposed property of the unicorn's horn will be explored in a later chapter.

There are two more classical European sources we should note, as they proved to be remarkably influential. Cosmas Indicopleustes in his *Topographica Christiana* describes a visit to Ethiopia (which he thought was in India) where he saw depictions of the unicorn in the emperor's palace. He wrote:

"This animal is called the unicorn, but I cannot say that I have seen him. But I have seen four brazen figures of him set up in the four-towered palace of the King of Ethiopia. From these figures I have been able to draw him as you see. They speak of him as a terrible beast and quite invincible and say that all his strength lies in his horn. When he finds himself pursued by many hunters and on the point of being caught, he springs up to the top of some precipice whence he throws himself down and in the descent turns a somersault so that the horn sustains all the shock of the fall, and he escapes unhurt." (*Cosmas Indicopleustes, Book 11*)

He drew a picture of an antelope as a quadruped with an upright horn and a collar around its neck to indicate that it belonged to the king. He had also seen a rhinoceros while in Ethiopia and describes it rather accurately, so he was certainly capable of describing what he saw.

Finally, one Julius Caesar, in his *De Bello Gallico*, wrote:

"There is an ox shaped like a stag, from the middle of whose forehead between the ears stands forth a single horn, taller and straighter than the horns we know. From its top branches spread out just like open hands. The main features of female and of male are the same, the same the shape and the size of the horns." (*Caesar, Book 6, Paragraph 26*)

Likely, what Julius Caesar described was a roe deer. Sometimes they grow a single antler in the middle of their head instead of two to either side. The picture below shows just such a deer in the early stages of antler growth. The palm-like branches described by Caesar are a good match to the branches of deer's antlers.

Figure 4. A young deer with growing antlers.

The ancient Greeks and Romans were not the only ones to write about unicorns. Some translations of Hebrew scriptures and scholarly writing also feature a unicorn. The beast, called a re'em, is referred to twice in Hebrew scripture (*Deuteronomy, Numbers*), in Hebrew scripture (*Isaiah, Job*) and in multiple Psalms. Until recently, there was some debate regarding the nature of the beast. In 1899, scholar Johan Duerst made the determination that the name re'em was represented in cuneiform by the sign ⟹, which means wild ox, or auroch in Hittite (*Duerst 7–8*).

You will note that there are two horns in the cuneiform symbol. This is important, as cuneiform is a descriptive language, in which the symbols visually represent the object being described. In his 1881 manuscript, Robert Brown Junior, Fellow of the Society of Antiquaries, Member of the Royal Astronomical Society, in advance of Duerst's scholarship, put forward that the cuneiform ideograph of re'em is the word for bull (*Brown, Section II*). Previously scholars had represented that ram, an animal that also has two horns, would be a better translation culturally than ox. We have no known cuneiform ideograph for unicorn, despite artistic representations of a unicorn found in archaeological sites.

Historically, until cuneiform was known and translated, Jewish scholars had presumed that re'em either represented a unicorn or a rhinoceros. In the Jerusalem Talmud, we find a curious debate between scholars who thought that the curtains that surrounded the Tabernacle were made of the multihued skins of unicorns, or of a single unicorn. Rabbi Yehudah believed the unicorn was an amazingly large kosher animal that was created just for the purpose of using the skin for the tabernacle curtain. Rabbi Nehemiah disagreed that the animal was kosher, and in other places the animal was not considered kosher (*Shurpin*).

Most important to the story of how the curtains of the tabernacle were created was that the creature came to Moses of its own volition. It sacrificed itself so that the tabernacle would have its hide as its curtains (*Shurpin*). I do homage to this debate in a scene within my novel, when Jewish surgeons debate if they can safely perform surgery on a unicorn as they are uncertain if the animal is kosher.

The unicorn is more than just one of the creatures of the tabernacle. Commonly depicted with a lion but not in the mutually

The Reality, Mythology, and Fantasies of Unicorns

antagonistic way it is depicted in other cultures' folklore, the unicorn is symbolic of Joseph, Jacob's son, the dreamer. Like the unicorn, Joseph wears a multicolored coat. Throughout Judaic scripture and folklore, this creature, the re'em, is associated with strength, and by associating the strength of the re'em with Joseph, the savior of both Egypt and the Hebrew peoples, they are asserting the strength of God's favor on the house of Jacob. The lion is one of Judaism's most enduring symbols, representing the majesty and strength of the tribe of Judah, the tribe from which the messiah will come.

The image in Figure 5 is from the sixteenth century ceiling painting in the Hodorov synagogue in Poland. That the lion seems to be placing the unicorn's horn into its mouth may be a reference to the use of ram's horns within Jewish ritual, especially to announce the holiest of holidays. Their limbs overlap in almost a cooperative dance under an archway that has birds and is surrounded by flowers, some of the same visual motifs used in Judaic art to indicate paradise.

Figure 5. The Lion and the Unicorn, a fragment of the 16th century ceiling painting in the Hodorov synagogue in Poland.

As nothing within any mythological tradition is constant, there is an equally compelling depiction of a unicorn and a lion that had been painted on the ceiling of the synagogue formerly located in Horb-am-Main, in 1735 CE. This painting shows the lion and the unicorn at strife, with the unicorn piercing the open mouth of the lion whose claws are trying to tear at the unicorn's legs. You can find this painting today in the Israel Museum in Jerusalem (*Beer, 76*).

Numerous references to what might be a unicorn in Hebraic scriptures frequently mention the strength of the beast. I'm going to use the King James and the Douay-Rheims translations of the scriptures, as they still mistranslate re'em to unicorn, rather than referring to the beast properly, as customary for the more modern and better translations into English. Contemporary Jewish translations consider the re'em to be a wild ox, as referenced in the text below.

To be clear, by wild ox they actually mean the species known to us as aurochs. This ancestor of all modern cattle became extinct in 1627. The definitive identification of re'em as auroch was made by Johann Ulrich Duerst, in his *Die Rinder von Babylonian, Assyrian and Agypten*. As most modern readers would have no clue what an auroch was, and even ancient authors would refer to the auroch as a wild ox, the use of wild ox probably makes the most sense.

Even the Douay-Rheims, which is an older translation of Judaeo-Christian scripture into English, preceding the King James, most often translates re'em as wild ox, not unicorn. The relevant mistranslations are: "God brought them out of Egypt; he hath as it were the strength of the unicorn." (*Numbers XXIII.22 KJV*), "His glory is like the firstling of his bullock, and his horns are like the horns of unicorns: with them he shall push the people together to the ends of the earth: and they are the ten thousands of Ephraim, and they are the thousands of Manasseh." (*Deuteronomy XXXIII.17 KJV*), "Will the unicorn be willing to serve thee, or abide by thy crib? Canst thou bind the unicorn with his band in the furrow? or will he harrow the valleys after thee? Wilt thou trust him, because his strength is great? or wilt thou leave thy labour to him?" (*Job XXXIX:9–11, KJV*).

Medieval Jewish scholars Yehudah HaLevi, Ibn Ezra, and Menasseh ben Israel all would have understood the re'em to be unicorn, however Saadia Gaon translated the word as Rhinoceros. (*Liebenberg, 21–27*) Others translate it as ram, a translation that fits the cultural context of the text in which the word is found, and the culture that produced the text. However, there are other known words for ram, so this translation is questionable, and likely was made by scholars who no longer had a reason to believe in unicorns.

Oddly enough, the Book of Daniel describes a battle between two creatures, one of which is described as a two-horned ram, the other as a one-horned goat. The one-horned goat wins out but breaks its horn, growing four in replacement (*Daniel, 8*). This is the only scriptural reference to a unicorn which cannot be explained away as being a reference to an auroch.

Finally, there is a Jewish folk tale regarding a unicorn and the trouble Noah had in getting it onto the Ark. In the tale, Og the demon begs to be rescued from the flood and produces a unicorn as a sign of his good faith. The unicorn is as large as a mountain, though Og says it is the smallest he could find. Noah eventually decides to lash the unicorn to the side of the ark. The size of the unicorn is reminiscent of the three-legged unicorn of Zoroastrianism, which we'll look at later in this chapter.

The Douay-Rheims does translate re'em as unicorn instead of as wild ox in its translation of Psalm 77 line 69 "and he built his sanctuary as of unicorns, in the land which he founded forever." (It is important to note that the Douay-Rheims translation has a slightly different numbering scheme for the Psalms than do many other translations. The Douay-Rheims numbering matches the Vulgate, the Septuagint, and the Coptic numbering schemes, while the King James and most modern translations match the numbering of Hebrew and Greek versions of the Psalms.)

The Greek and Coptic translation of Psalm 21 also refers to the unicorn. "Rescue my soul from the sword, and from a dog's flaw my only lift! Save me from a lion's mouth, and my lowliness from the horns of unicorns!" (*NETS translation of the Septuagint, Psalm 21, 21–22*). I'll come back to this at some length in the next chapter as we look less at history and archaeology and more at the mythologies associated with the unicorn.

Medieval Jews are not the only ones who associate the unicorn with God's holy sanctuary. The re'em was commonly thought by medieval European Christian scholars to be a unicorn, based upon the ancient Greek source of their scripture which translated re'em as unicorn. This trend was preserved in the Latin translations of the scripture used by the western branches of Christianity. Medieval European scholars of both Jewish and Christian religions would not only look to their own scripture for inspiration of their unicorn myth, they often looked to the fragments of surviving Ancient Greek histories.

One other ancient author was often quoted by the Medieval Europeans regarding their beliefs about the unicorn. Oppian, in a poem on the art of hunting, writes of a beast with solid hooves and a single horn inhabiting Boeotia.

The unicorn is written about in histories and bestiaries as a real animal found in the wilds of foreign lands. The existence of the unicorn in medieval Europe was taken for granted. However, bestiaries kept hanging fantastic properties on the horn of the unicorn, but they were not the only source of fancy regarding the unicorn. One also finds multiple poets writing about the unicorn.

The medieval poet Pfaffen Lamprecht added another detail to the growing myth of the unicorn; according to his poem *Alexanderlied*, it had a ruby under its horn. He writes:

> "I had from this rich queen
> A beast of proud and noble mien
> That bears in his brow the ruby-stone
> And yields himself to maids alone.
> But few such unicorns are found
> On this or any other ground,
> And only such are ever captured
> As stainless virgins have enraptured." (*Shepard, 82*)

Eschenbach copied this idea in his poem, *Parzival*:

> "We caught the beast called Unicorn
> That knows and loves a maiden best
> And falls asleep upon her breast;
> We took from underneath his horn
> The splendid male carbuncle-stone
> Sparkling against the white skull-bone." (*Shepard, 82*)

Not all the descriptive fancy was about the horn, the shape or size of the beast, though there is enough about the horn of the unicorn that we'll take a closer look at it in a later chapter.

At the end of the prose romance, *Le Chevalier du Papegau*, a dwarf tells King Arthur of how, soon after the death of his wife in childbirth, the dwarf found a hollow tree with six unicorn fawns. The mother, upon her return to the den, took pity on his crying child and fed him from one of its fourteen udders (*Shepard, 86*).

The medieval Islamic world, much like that of medieval Judaism, was less isolated than that of medieval Christianity, which itself was less isolated than commonly thought. Not only did medieval Islamic scholars have access to the legends and texts of the ancient Greeks, Hebrews, and Romans, but many other cultures influenced and participated in the formation of medieval Islam. As with medieval Judaism, some of the literature referring to a unicorn is confused with that referring to the rhinoceros. However, you can find creatures that are obviously unicorns, and not rhinoceros, clearly depicted in their history, literature, and art.

Unlike in medieval Christianity or Judaism, the unicorn in the Islamic world was not necessarily a creature that was horse- or goat-like. There are depictions of winged unicorns with feline bodies found in Islamic art in medieval Syria, Iran, Morocco, and Spain. Art from the Sejulk Turks shows such feline unicorns hunting elephants and other creatures. Ferocious beasts indeed. Depictions of antelope-like unicorns are called khutu, karkadan, karkaddan, and kardunn. The word karkadan is sometimes also used for the rhinoceros (*Ettinghausen 6–8*).

On an enameled Syrian glass vessel of the fourteenth century, currently housed in the Freer Gallery of Art, you see two griffins, two sphinxes, a winged lion, and three winged unicorns. Another Syrian vessel from the thirteenth century shows winged unicorns, but more importantly, it also shows animals with two horns, indicating that the drawing of the unicorn with a single horn was deliberate. In both cases the head and body are like that of a horse (*Ettinghausen, 3*).

It is important to note that depictions of the karkadan as a unicorn without wings is found in Islamic art, though the unicorn, with or without wings, was not a frequent motif. Much of the variation in depiction comes from literary sources. I'll make reference only to those descriptions that are clearly not of the rhinoceros, a beast encountered by a number of Islamic authors both in India and in Africa. Al-Damiri writes of the unicorn as a hybrid of an elephant and horse. Al-Zamakhshari, in his discussion of whether or not the meat of the karkadan could be lawfully eaten, has much the same view of the creature.

Shah-namah, the Iranian book of Kings, describes the karkadan (called a karg within the text) as having the claws of a lion. Al-Jawhari and Al-Damiri also describe the karkadan has having the claws of a lion. Al-Tawhidi, Al-Qazwini, and Al-Mustawifi all describe the karkadan as small, the size of a goat kid (*Ettinghausen*).

Some authors, like Al-Jāhiz, quote Aristotle when they describe the karkadan as having the horn in the middle of the forehead. The horn they describe is long, often one or two cubits in length, pointed, and harder than the tusks of an elephant. Ibn Fadlān wrote, "the animal is smaller than the camel and bigger than the bull. The head is that of a camel, its tail that of a bull, and its body that of a mule. Its feet are like the hoofs of the bull. In the middle of its head it has a single, thick and round horn which becomes thinner towards the top." (*Ettinghausen, 13*)

When describing a karkadan, Al-Qazwini says the karkadan has the body of an elephant. Al-Damiri indicated that it was a cross between a horse and an elephant. A 1514 manuscript by Al-Qazwini, an Iranian author, describes a karkadan with a hump on its back, as well as certain elephantine features (*Ettinghausen, 14*). Knowing that elasmotherium had what would have been described as a hump on its back makes me wonder if they are describing elasmotherium, perhaps from memory if not from observation.

In Islamic lore, there is a second kind of unicorn, the shadhaver. The shadhaver, according to Al-Qazwini and Al-Damiri, is found in Rûm, what is today modern Turkey. It is a unicorn that looks like a gazelle, but its horn has forty-two hollow branches. When it runs, or when the wind passes through those branches, the shadhaver's horn makes a pleasant sound (*Ettinghausen, 64*). While both the shadhaver and the karkadan are described as being associated with music, the karkadan is often depicted as a fierce beast, attacking lions, elephants, and other creatures (*Ettinghausen, 29*).

According to Al-Jāhiz, the karkadan is so rare because its gestation period is as long as that of an elephant, making it among the least abundant of beasts (*Ettinghausen, 52*). If, however, Chevalier du Papegau is correct on the number of udders, they must have been fertile creatures. Before it is born, the fetus sticks its head out from its mother and eats the branches of trees, pulling back its head when satisfied (*Ettinghausen, 16*). This would make the unicorn a marsupial.

There is another kind of unicorn known within Islamic lore, the harish. According to Al-Tawhidi, the harish is small, about the size of a lamb, but is fierce and strong. The only way to capture it is to expose it to a young virgin. It will leap into her arms, as if intending to suckle. The harish is so intoxicated by this desire that it can be tied up firmly with a rope. A different account, the Manafi' Al-Hayawan, gets around the inherent difficulty of trying to suckle milk from the breast of a virgin by substituting her with a beautiful woman from a brothel who is infinitely more likely to be able to produce milk (*Ettinghausen, 60*).

Fans of Monty Python will be delighted with the next type of Islamic unicorn. The Al-miraj is a unicorn hare which is fierce and attacks all creatures who run from it in terror. However, when threatened, the unicorn will leap off a precipice, land on its horn, do a summersault, and escape unhurt. This behavior has been observed in the Persian wild goat, as fanciful as it sounds (*Ettinghausen, 66; Al-Qazwini, 131*).

Unicorns in China are known as ki-lin, kiren, qi-lin, or qi-lin, depending upon the transliteration (pronounced "chi-lin" in Mandarin Chinese). Unlike in western texts, where unicorns are somewhat confused with the rhinoceros, early literature and de-

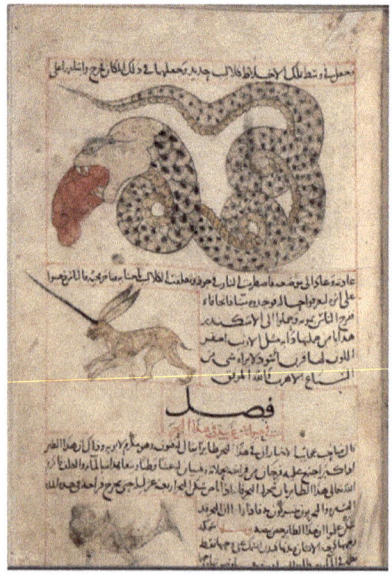

Figure 6. Al-miraj and Serpent.

pictions of the qilin are often describing a creature much like a giraffe. In Korean and Japanese, the same word is used for both unicorn and giraffe. This confusion comes from the Emperor Wu of Han, and from Zheng He's journey to West Africa. Zheng He returned with a pair of giraffes, which the Emperor proclaimed to be qilin and proof of the greatness of his power. In modern Chinese, the word used for unicorn is dújiǎoshòu, to avoid any confusion.

The qilin is thought to be a resident of heaven, and is only seen on earth at momentous events or when they bring messages from the gods. The first known sighting of the qilin was in the palace of the Emperor Huang-di. A qilin brought a jade tablet to the mother of Confucius just before the sage's birth, proclaiming to her the greatness of the son she bore. In the hopes

Figure 7. Qilin.

that their children would also be great, many women's quarters in traditional China had pictures of qilin. To say to someone that a qilin appeared at their birth is still a high compliment.

Unlike the unicorn in the west, the qilin is neither ferocious nor hunted. It eats no living thing and won't tread on an insect nor on a blade of grass. Also, unlike the unicorn in the west, there is no tradition of the horn of the qilin having curative properties, and it is not sought after in traditional medicine. Like the unicorn in the west, the qilin is a solitary creature.

In Chinese literature, unlike Islamic, Christian, or Judaic writings, there is no confusing the qilin with the rhinoceros. Rhinoceros horns had clear medicinal value in traditional Chinese medicine, and their horns were prized charms.

Ghengis Khan's biographer told of how a qilin prevented Ghengis Khan from going forward with his plans to invade Nepal and India. The qilin appeared before Ghengis Khan, did homage to him, but stood squarely in the path of the Khan and his army. Ghengis Khan took the hint and never brought the Golden Horde into India. In my novel *The Garden at the Roof of the World*, I use this tale of respite from the terrors of Ghengis Khan and his army to explain why the King of Nepal is so eager to help a unicorn and those who accompany it.

A Chinese traveler, whose name has not come down to us, reported about eighty qilin in Tibet. In this remote region, unicorn sightings continued in the modern era, with the Rajah of Bootan convincing Captain Samuel Turner that he had once possessed a unicorn, and Major Latter of the British army wrote home about sighting a unicorn in Tibet in 1820. I'll explore this in more detail in a later chapter.

Much of Indian lore regarding the unicorn is found in Islamic stories about the karkadan which I've already covered. Unicorns are also found in medieval Hindu and Buddhist art. One of the oldest depictions of a unicorn in art comes from ancient seals found in the Indus River valley.

Strikingly, the head of the unicorn in the seal (see Figure 8) looks much like the reconstructions of elasmotherium. The animal, called a ṛṣya in ancient Sanskrit, is portrayed with a curved horn that has ridges on it. The neck is long, like that of an ass or a horse, which matches the descriptions of the unicorn being similar to a large ass you find in Ctesias' writing. If you compare this seal with others of the period and region, you find the seals of bull and deer are very accurate in their details, so it is to be expected that this seal also shows an animal accurately. However, as other seals depict animals with multiple heads and tigers with horns, it is possible that this depiction of a unicorn just illustrates a myth. There is reason to think that the seal may depict an actual animal that lived once upon a time. Scholars think that the language in the seal is likely proto-Dravidian, not Sanskrit. There are over 600 known symbols, much like the cuneiform in use in contemporary Mesopotamia.

Every unicorn seal found to date includes an image of a brazier set on a pedestal. This object has a bowl-like shape and is not often found in the seals depicting other animals. Also, such unicorn seals often contain an image of an object that is either box-like or drum-like, set on a pedestal and sometimes represented with a handle for carrying. While no such object has survived, this could well be a depiction of a vessel used in a Vedic ritual which I'll discuss later in this chapter. Unfortunately, the archaeologists don't make reference to the Vedic literature in their examination of the symbols on the unicorn seals. They speculate on what these objects might be without reference to the known rituals.

Indus Valley seals depict known animals with accuracy, and the fantastic creatures portrayed in these images are always composed of actual animal features and forms. One is a man whose hindquarters extend into those of a tiger, bearing some semblance to a centaur, with the torso of a man set on a body of a beast.

The tiger-person has thick, long tresses of hair with characteristics of the markhor, an animal native to India, though in the image there are also what appear to be plants in its hair. The front legs appear to be clothed, while the rear legs are that of a tiger. Some scholars think this creature may have been a link to the Assyrian goddess Ishtar (or Inanna, in Sumerian) who was associated with lions. The Harappan civilization was a contemporary to the Akkadian period of Mesopotamia when Ishtar was worshiped. However, the figure on the seal doesn't appear to be female, and the beastly half is a tiger, not a lion, so the connection is tenuous at best.

Terracotta statues of a unicorn bull with a hole in its belly that have been found in the Indus Valley indicate that such statures were most likely carried on a stick in some form of ritual or show.

Figure 8. Indus Valley seal.

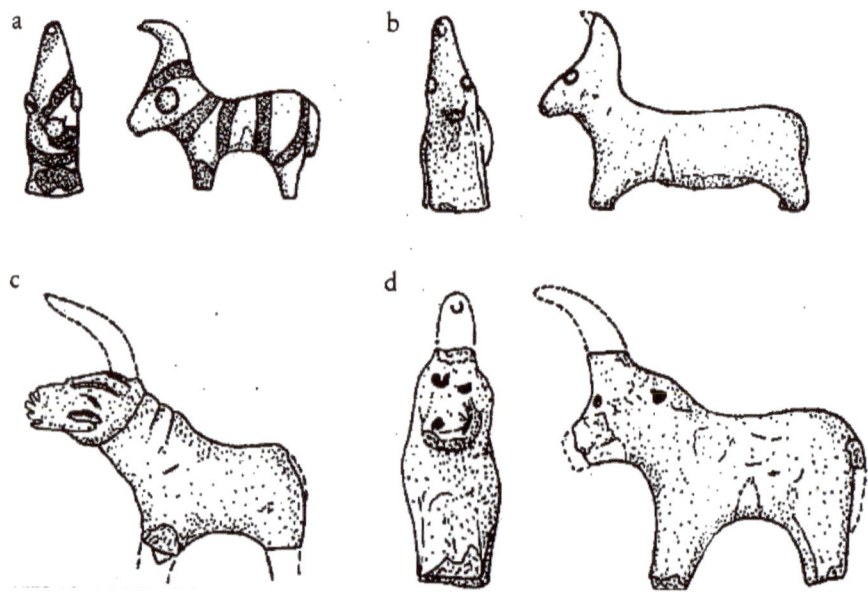

Figure 9. Unicorn figurine found at Chanhu-daro.

There is one unique tablet from Mohenjo-daro that shows a procession with a unicorn image carried on a high standard, as if it represented some deity or sacred emblem (*Caspers, 328*).

The image in Figure 9 is one of the five unicorn figurines found in Chanhu-daro. Some were also found at Mohenjo-daro and Harappa. The clay figurine has a red band spiraling around its body and eyes which end at the base of the single horn. The horn curves forward and the snout is long and narrow. Again, the beast is similar to our reconstructions of elasmotherium. However, since the front and back legs are joined together, it is possible that the creator chose to represent two horns the same way they represented the two pairs of legs. There is a hole in the belly for the figurine to be mounted on a stick.

This depiction links the unicorn more closely to the cult of Ishtar/Inanna, as statues excavated from the city of Mari on the Euphrates, which were believed to be used in a Mesopotamian victory parade, included that of a unicorn bull carried on the top of a stand (*Parpola, 438*). It is important to remember that Ishtar/Inanna was the goddess of both sex and war.

Figure 10. Procession of unicorns and lions from Persepolis.

One final image links the unicorn to the cult of Ishtar rather conclusively. Figure 10 depicts both lions (a known symbol of Ishtar/Inanna) and unicorns walking in parallel paths separated by rosettes, which were also a known symbol of the Ishtar/Inanna cult.

THE REALITY, MYTHOLOGY, AND FANTASIES OF UNICORNS

Figure 11. One of a number of figures from a victory parade panel from the Ishtar temple at Mari.

The image in Figure 11 shows a statue from a collection that depicts the Assyrian New Year's military parade, complete with the unicorn on a pedestal.

You also find references to a unicorn in the Zoroastrian religion. One of the precepts of Zoroastrianism is that everything is either pure or impure. The impure animals tend to be those that are dangerous to humans, such as the snake or the lion. Pure animals include those that are beneficial to humans, such as the bull. In *The Sacred Liturgy and Gathas/Hymns of Zarathushtra* as translated by L.H. Mills (section 42, which is a supplement to the *Haptanghaiti*), we find this hymn:

> We worship You, O Ye Bountiful Immortals! the entire collection of this Yasna, Haptanghaiti (as we sum up all). And we

sacrifice to the fountains of the waters, and to the fordings of the rivers, to the forkings of the highways, and to the meetings of the roads.

And we sacrifice to the hills that run with torrents, and the lakes that brim with waters! and to the corn that fills the cornfields; and we sacrifice to both the protector and the Creator, to both Zarathushtra and the Lord.

And we sacrifice to both earth and heaven, and to the stormy wind that Mazda made, and to the peak of high Haraiti, and to the land, and all things good.

And we worship the Good Mind (in the living) and the spirits of the saints. And we sacrifice to the fish of fifty-fins, and to that sacred beast the Unicorn which stands in Vouru-kasha, and we sacrifice to that sea of Vouru-kasha where he stands, and to the Haoma, golden-flowered, growing on the heights; yea, to the Haoma that restores us, and aids this world's advance. We sacrifice to Haoma that driveth death afar, (6) and to the flood-streams of the waters, and to the great flights of the birds, and to the approaches of the Fire-priests, as they approach us from afar, and seek to gain the provinces, and spread the ritual lore. And we sacrifice to the Bountiful Immortals all!

There is another reference to a one-horned creature in Zoroastrianism. Chapter 19 of *The Bundahis* refers to a three-legged ass which has one horn, two ears, nine mouths, and six eyes. In the L.H. Mills translation of Chapter 19, we learn:

The one horn is as it were of gold and hollow, and a thousand branch horns have grown upon it, some befitting a camel, some befitting a horse, some befitting an ox, some befitting an ass, both great and small. With that horn it will vanquish and dissipate all the vile corruption due to the efforts of noxious creatures.

This is another source of the idea that the horn of a unicorn can dispel poison. We'll examine this in a later chapter.

There is considerable scholarship linking the Ishtar and the older Inanna cults of Mesopotamia to that of the cult of Durga in India. Much like Ishtar/Inanna, Durga was celebrated with an annual military parade. In the Indus Valley and ancient Mesopotamia, they carried clay statues of unicorns in those parades. The Vedic precursor to this parade included a story of the sexual union of a celibate bard and a prostitute.

The Reality, Mythology, and Fantasies of Unicorns

Many scholars believe that the worship of Ishtar and Inanna included the use of sacred prostitution in the new year's ritual, the very ritual parade in which a unicorn statue on a pedestal was featured. Considering the nature of the myth of the unicorn in medieval Christianity, that the unicorn in ancient Mesopotamia was associated with the goddess of love and war is more than a trifle ironic. However, this does explain certain aspects of the unicorn story that survived in the depiction of the hunt for the unicorn, as will be explored in a later chapter.

It is the link between Durga and the unicorn that I explored in my own novel, *The Garden at the Roof of the World*. In the Hindu epic *The Devi Mahatmyam*, Durga summons Kali from within herself to destroy the demon Raktabija, which Kali accomplishes. While Kali is considered the destroyer, she destroys so that spring and hope may return. Inspired by the link between Durga and the unicorn, I have the goddess Kali in my novel working with Kavundi, who is a sannyasi (a Hindu nun). She helps bring my characters to the garden at the roof of the world (based on the myth of the Shambhala) where they aim to save the life of the unicorn who walked with the first woman in paradise.

When you examine the Indus Valley seals showing known animals, they are strikingly realistic for the size of the image. Of importance, the carvings are clearly aimed to be accurate. Even when the animal is shown in profile, if it has two horns, they are rendered in a manner to be quite visible. Often, the seal carvings of such beasts also include depictions of foods consumed by the animal. Unlike the carvings of the composite beasts of myth found in other Indus Valley seals, these images are very realistic. There is no human torso or head, or other supernatural elements. With this knowledge, it seems significant that the unicorn image is the most commonly found motif in Indus Valley seals. The seals themselves are made from dolomitic steatite that has been heated to temperatures in excess of 1200 degrees Celsius to transform them into whitened enstatite. This indicates a culture with sophisticated technology and involves a significant amount of resources into the production of these seals.

There is sufficient diversity in the styling and textual labeling associated with the unicorn seals of the Indus Valley to indicate multiple interconnected workshops or schools,

Figure 12. Statite stamp with human-headed composite creature with bovine horns from Mohenjo-daro.

potentially situated in different regions. If we ever gain the ability to translate the text, we may be able to clarify that issue.

There is one more connection to be explored between the Indus Valley and Mesopotamia, which speaks to frequent commerce. Two beads found in Mesopotamia associated with the Sumerian king Shulgi at the end of the third millennium BCE apparently were of Indus Valley origin. The production and use of beads was a thriving industry in the Harappan civilization. The one bead is made of a translucent red stone, facetted to form a hexagon in section, likely rubbed down from a less convenient shape into one upon which they could carve the cuneiform inscription to the goddess Bau. Another is a pierced bead shaped like a fine pale red and yellow translucent cylinder. Bau was the goddess of dogs and the daughter of the Sumerian god Anu.

Earlier I mentioned that there is an ancient Vedic ritual that may have involved the unicorn. A careful reading of the text shows that the ritual involved the use of two unicorn horns bound together to form a parīśāsau—a handle used to carry an earthenware vessel filled with molten metal. The Vedic

The Reality, Mythology, and Fantasies of Unicorns

literature indicated that this was because the unicorn horn was the only material strong enough to bear the heat of the earthenware vessel, which was hot enough to hold the molten metal in ritual imitation of solar heat. According to these texts, unicorn horns are ideal material for this purpose because, unlike the horns of a bull or a rhinoceros, they are not hollow nor short. Their undulating shape makes them perfect to wrap around the earthenware vessel.

Two things that are interesting to note. First, the word parīśāsa has a double meaning: not only does it mean horn, but it also means weapon or knife. The second is that the picture of the unicorn on the Indus Valley seals shows the beast with an undulating horn. This makes it more likely that the seal depicts the creature whose horn was used in the ancient Vedic ritual.

There are two interesting Indian myths that include unicorns. In one variation of the *Mahābhārata*, an ancient sacred epic of India, you find a unicorn boar. This boar is an avatar of Vishnu. The text, in translation, reads, "Having assumed, in the past, the form of a boar with a single horn, of a divine aspect, I raised this (submerged) Earth. Therefore I am the unicorn." It is always possible that the translation to boar is a modern corruption of the original meaning, or that the elasmotherium looked more like a boar to the ancient and unknown poet.

In a Buddhist story, the *Mahāvastu*, we find a one-horned sage who is the offspring of a female doe. This sage, when tempted to return to civilization by women, brings much-needed rain. We also find a remarkable hymn that is inspired by an interesting passage in the first volume of the *Mahāvastu*. In the section entitled *The History of the Deer Park*, five hundred Pratyekabuddhas each recited a verse and passed away. The last line of each verse has been sometimes translated as "let one live in loneliness like a unicorn."[i]

The hymn itself is lovely and is often quoted. My personal favorite quote is found on a powerful print of a unicorn hunt in India, engraved by J. Collaert. The image shows four unicorns charging a group of archers who are shooting at the unicorns, slaying one of them. The hymn is:

Like a lion, without fear of the howling pack,
    Like a gust of wind, ne'er trapped in a snare,

---

i https://www.ancient-buddhist-texts.net/Reference/Early-Buddhist-Texts/03-EBT-Mahavastu.htm

Like a lotus blossom, ne'er sprinkled by water,
Let me, like a unicorn, in solitude roam.
(*Beer, 14*)

Like with most scripture, there is little evidence that Buddha himself uttered that prayer. It is, however, found in one of the oldest Buddhist manuscripts, the *Mahāvastu*, which dates from between the second to fourth centuries CE. This text is the primary source of the idea of the transcendent Buddha. While similar to the much older Pāli Canon, there are significant differences in more than just theology, which represent the change in the religion in the two hundred years between the authorship of the texts.

There is one more description of the unicorn from India. In this case, it is a medieval one from the Italian traveler Marco Polo. He writes:

> "When you quit the kingdom of Ferlec you enter upon that of Basma. This also is an independent kingdom, and the people have a language of their own... There are wild elephants in the country, and numerous unicorns, which are very nearly as big. They have hair like that of a buffalo, feet like those of an elephant, and a horn in the middle of the forehead, which is black and very thick. They do no mischief, however, with the horn, but with the tongue alone; for this is covered all over with long and strong prickles [and when savage with any one they crush him under their knees and then rasp him with their tongue]. The head resembles that of a wild boar, and they carry it ever bent towards the ground. They delight much to abide in mire and mud. 'Tis a passing ugly beast to look upon, and is not in the least like that which our stories tell of as being caught in the lap of a virgin; in fact, 'tis altogether different from what we fancied. There are also monkeys here in great numbers and of sundry kinds; and goshawks as black as crows. These are very large birds and capital for fowling."

Marco Polo may have been a bigot, and he certainly looked down on those he encountered with a sneer; however, his descriptions of places and beasts is generally accurate. The beast he described is not the Indian rhinoceros, which has a single horn, but not the thick hair, boar like head, nor are their horns in the middle of their forehead.

Is it possible that some of the elasmotherium survived long enough for Marco Polo to see them in Basma, India, in the fourteenth century? It is, though we have no direct archaeological evidence. The description Marco Polo gives matches the picture on the Indus seal. Some of it even matches the description given by Ctesias of Cnidus and Glaudius Aelianus. The archaeological record is rich, but far from complete. Not finding something in the archaeological record is not an indication of its absence in the historical record.

Since elasmotherium was discovered, we have known that unicorns were not just a figure of myth and legend. We don't know when the species became extinct, but it is as likely as not that in the midst of Marco Polo's journey home, he beheld the true unicorn in Basma, India, and was amazed at the discrepancy between the myth he knew and the reality he was confronting. It is also possible that he saw the one-horned Indian rhino and completely misdescribed the shape, hide, and coloring of the beast, which is the common assumption. I prefer to think that Marco Polo described what he saw with accuracy, and that elasmotherium was with us through the mid to late thirteenth century.

THE MYTH OF THE ENDLESS BATTLE BETWEEN THE LION AND THE UNICORN

There are three main myths involving the unicorn. There is the myth of the unicorn's endless battle with the lion, the myth on how to successfully hunt for a unicorn, and the myths of curative properties of the horn. I will deal with each of these mythologies in this and in the next two chapters.

The myth of the unicorn's endless battle can be found in Spenser's poetry, in British nursery rhymes, in artwork, and in heraldry. I'll start with heraldry, which will lead to an exploration of what art and archaeology seem to reveal regarding the nature of the unicorn's endless battle with the lion.

For those who are not experts, it would be beneficial to review the heraldic symbols before discussing how the unicorn is depicted. As there are entire books on the subject, I'm going to be both brief and concise regarding identifying common symbols. Each of the colors used in traditional European heraldry has a symbolic element. Gold, also called or, is a symbol of the sun, power and splendor. Silver, also called argent, symbolizes the moon, peace, and sincerity. Black, also called sable, symbolizes Saturn, constancy, and sometimes, grief. Blue, also called azure, symbolizes Venus, truth, and loyalty. Brown, also called maroon, symbolizes patience in battle. Green, also called vert, symbolizes mercury, hope, and joy. Purple, also called purpure, denotes royalty and majesty. Orange, also called tawney, symbolizes worthy ambition and work. Finally, there is red, also known as gules, which symbolizes Mars, the military, and fortitude.

Robert Brown, in his 1881 book *The Unicorn, a Mythological Investigation*, gives us a clear view into the use of the unicorn as a heraldic symbol. Brown claims that the unicorn is a lunar symbol, based on the fact that it's always depicted in silver, while the lion is a solar symbol, since it's universally depicted in gold. The duality reinforces the notion that the two are antithetical to each other. As the moon rules the sea and water, so the unicorn's horn is thought to purify water with its touch. As the Ancient Greek goddess of the moon, Artemis is chaste and virginal, so the unicorn is attracted to those women who are chaste or virginal. Brown goes to great lengths to show that many cultures have identified the sun with a lion, the moon with the unicorn. In one of his sources, Gesner's *History of Animals*, the unicorn and the lion are enemies by nature. When a unicorn sees a lion, it charges. To escape, the lion climbs a tree, which the unicorn in its fury will stab, as it is unable to swerve from its course in its attempt to slay the lion. The lion will then drop on the unicorn, whose horn is stuck in the tree, and destroy it. (*Brown, 61*)

The unicorn first appears as an emblem of the Scottish royal family in the time of Robert II or Robert III. We have two gold coins from that era with the emblem of the unicorn. James III of Scotland also issued similar coins.

As for the nursery rhyme, this likely is a reference to the use of the lion as the heraldic emblem of the monarchy of England, and the unicorn as the heraldic emblem of the monarchy of Scotland. The rhyme is as follows:

> The lion and the unicorn
> Were fighting for the crown
> The lion beat the unicorn
> All around the town
> Some gave them white bread
> And some gave them brown
> Some gave them plum cake
> And drummed them out of town
> And when he had beat him out,
> He beat him in again;
> He beat him three times over
> His power to maintain

There is also a description of the contest in Spenser's *Faerie Queen*:

> Like as the lyon, whose imperial powre
> A proud rebellious unicorn defyes,
> T'avoide the rash assault and wrathful stowre
> Of his fiers foe, him to a tree applies.
> And when him running in full course he spyes
> He slips aside; the whiles that furious beast
> His precious horne, sought of his enimyes,
> Strikes in the stroke, ne thence can be released,
> But to the victor yields a bounteous feast.

The royal houses of England and Scotland fought with each other throughout many centuries. They were not to be formally unified into a single kingdom until the reign of Queen Anne. The royal crest of both England and Scotland has born the symbols of both kingdoms since the rule of James I of England, who was also James VI of Scotland. It is somewhat ironic that while the rhyme has the lion always winning, in the end a Scottish king sat on the thrones of both kingdoms. Thus, the unicorn won out, at least in the United Kingdom.

Brown claims that two particular crests have preserved an older heraldic message regarding the unicorn. The crest of the Bickerstaff family shows a unicorn nightly triumphant over the sun, by depicting the sun with sable rays surmounted by a unicorn. Even more curious is the crest of the Curteis family, where a unicorn is shown between four trees, which Brown (*62*) claimed was a mythological allusion to the grove of the underworld.

You find the unicorn and the lion frequently in the iconography of lands far from the conflict between England and Scotland, and they are not always fighting. Brown was likely unaware that the famous Cossack chief Yermak, who conquered Siberia in 1581, carried three standards, that of a dove, a lion, and a unicorn. You can also find in the Oruzheinaia Palata the account of an ivory throne presented as a wedding gift from the last Emperor of the Roman Empire (known to us as the Byzantine Empire) on the occasion of the marriage of Ivan III of Russia to the Emperor's niece, Zoe. One side of the throne bears the carving of a lion, on the other that of a unicorn. Above the lion is carved a dove, and on the top, the two-headed eagle. The two-headed eagle had been the symbol of the Byzantine Imperial family in the later centuries of the Empire, and would become the symbol of the Imperial family of Russia (*Bunt, 428*).

The lion and the unicorn are also found peaceably co-existing in a Byzantine manuscript of the *Proverbs of Solomon* from the fifteenth century. This manuscript contains a drawing of a youth standing between the branches of a tree, eating a fig. Higher up in the tree there are two parrots and two storks, and lower down there is a lion on one side, a unicorn on the other, and two mice in the center at the roots of the tree, one white, one black (*Bunt, 428*). This seems to be an illustration loosely inspired by a Buddhist story, the *Mahabharata*, though many of the particulars have been changed from the original. An image referring to the same story is also found on a bronze door in the Uspenski Monastery of Aleksandrov, Russia, dated to 1336. In the story in the *Proverbs of Solomon*, a man is chased into a pit by a unicorn, and he hangs onto a tree for his safety. Below him, a lion is eagerly waiting for his demise, however the man is happy for the moment, due to the delicious fruit on the tree he is holding on to. His situation remains perilous, because at the base of the tree, the mice are eating away at the trunk. The tree will eventually topple over, and he shall fall into the jaws of the waiting lion. While this scene is certainly a metaphor for the fragility of the joys of life, it also likely contains a deeper metaphor, about being caught between two powerful nations. While Al-Qazwini presumed that unicorns could be found in Rûm,[i] I could find no other reference that would classify the unicorn as one of the symbols of the Roman Empire in the medieval era (*Ettinghausen, 64–66*).

You also find the lion and the unicorn peacefully co-existing in Roman artifacts. A Roman plate found in 1830 in Berthouville, France, had animals painted on the rim, including a lion and a unicorn. The plate has been dated to sometime in the first three hundred years of the Roman Empire (*Bunt, 432*).

The lion and the unicorn are more often found in conflict with each other. An ivory casket of Syrian or Egyptian workmanship dated to the eleventh or twelfth century CE, currently held in

---

i   The Empire we call Byzantine was called by its citizens and contemporaries the Roman Empire. The name Byzantine was given to the Empire by scholars who saw a clear cultural break with the older Roman Empire and decided not to respect how the leaders, citizens, and contemporaries referred to the Empire.

the Kaiser Friedrich Museum in Berlin, shows a lion grabbing a unicorn by the flanks. This motif is typical for the Middle Eastern art featuring the lion and the unicorn (*Bunt, 430*).

An Ancient Greek relief from the fourth century BCE, displayed in the Hermitage, St. Petersburg, Russia, shows the goddess Cybele, with a lion and a unicorn in combat portrayed at the bottom (*Bunt, 433*). By now, it is plain that there is a relationship between the lion and the unicorn that crosses many countries and goes back many centuries. However, despite numerous portrayals of their battles, it is not always an antagonistic relationship.

On the famous horn of Ulf (named after the Viking prince who used to own it and currently housed in York, UK), you find a carving of Hekate Triformis with three animals, one of which is a unicorn. Some believe the horn was carved from an elephant tusk in Salerno, Italy. An inscription on the horn states that Ulphus, Prince of the western parts of Deira gave it to the church of St. Peter, along with all his lands and revenues. The other animals in the carving on the horn include a dog and a serpent. Brown claims that the unicorn represents the crescent moon, the serpent the full moon, and the dog represents the half moon, or perhaps the new moon. The prominent eye of the unicorn on the horn, according to Brown (*45*), is an indication that the moon is waxing and soon will be full.

Shephard gives a richer description of the carving on the horn, which he describes as Byzantine in origin. The unicorn is touching the tree with its horn. While its head is somewhat equine, the body and legs are that of a bull, and the tail is a serpent. Beneath the belly, there emerges the head of the dog. There is a lion on the horn, but it is leaping on a fawn, not on the unicorn (*Shephard, 250*). Unfortunately, there is no precise dating of the age of the horn itself.

Hekate was closely linked in ancient times to Erishkigal, the Sumerian goddess of the underworld who was known as the Queen of the Night. There is an ancient Greek hymn to Hekate Erishkigal (*Betz, 287–295*). Hecate was a chthonic goddess, able to pass the gates between realms and unlock the gates of death. The entrance to hell is described by the poet Virgil as Hecate's grove, thus the reason that Brown believes the trees in the Curteis family crest would have been the entrance to the underworld (*Brown, 62*).

The Reality, Mythology, and Fantasies of Unicorns

Erishkigal, the Sumerian and Assyrian goddess of the underworld and Queen of the Night was the sister to the goddess Ishtar/Inanna. Both Erishkigal and Ishtar/Inanna were daughters of the moon god, which backs up Brown's thesis that the unicorn is a lunar symbol. I only know of one surviving image depicting Erishkigal from ancient Mesopotamia: a clay relief figurine believed to be a representation of Erishkigal (Figure 13).

This clay figurine is thought to be Erishkigal because of the two owls to either side of the figure of the goddess; however, the relief also depicts lions, making this identification problematic

Figure 13. Queen of the Night.

as lions are a known symbol of Ishtar/Inanna and it is not uncommon to find images of Ishtar/Inanna standing on lions. The rivalry between unicorns and lions could go all the way back to the rivalry between the Sumerian goddesses Inanna and Erishkigal, the Sumerian Queen of heaven and the Sumerian Queen of the night. I'll explore this a bit more later in this chapter.

Not all mythologists are content with the idea of the unicorn as a lunar symbol. Elmer Suhr (*108*) links the grooved horn of the unicorn to a solar phenomenon, that of the solar eclipse. The colors associated with the unicorn by Ctesias and Aelian are all observed in the corona of the sun during the eclipse. The eye of the moon's shadow can be likened to the foot of an elephant, though it passes over water as easily as land. The horn resembles a cone-shaped shadow. Even the notion of the unicorn fleeing from a predator, leaping off a cliff, and bouncing on its horn to land on its feet can be imagined from how the shadow of the eclipse will fall off a cliff point-first. So, the unicorn isn't a lunar symbol per se, just the symbol of the solar eclipse, and the battle between the unicorn and the lion that always ends with the lion winning is a reassuring tale that the sun will always overcome the eclipse, which will be temporary.

Much like the unicorn's horn is thought to cure poison, there are ancient myths claiming the moon itself can cure poison, but only some of the time. According to these myths, the waxing moon swells and grows in purity, making everything thrive, while during the waning of the moon, impure and poisonous things become more potent (*Shepard, 244*). In Ptolemy's *Tetrabiblon*, we learn that the moon's influence comes from it being closer to the earth than other heavenly bodies, so it can draw vapors from the earth itself. While the Arabian astrologer Alburmasar doubted this, as the moon was too high, Cardan supported Ptolemy by claiming that the moon's pull was like that of a magnet to iron.

Brown builds his case of the unicorn as a lunar symbol by looking extensively at ancient art from the near east. The first he mentions is an Assyrian sardonyx seal in the Louvre, Paris, which depicts a crowned person, likely a king, grabbing a dagger in his right hand. To his left is a unicorn goat standing on its hind legs, its horn touching a tree. Above the unicorn is carved a crescent moon. The king is poised to strike and kill the unicorn with the dagger.

Another he mentions is a Babylonian gem, also showing a king grasping a dagger to kill a crowned goat in exactly the same position as the unicorn goat in the Assyrian seal. There is a moon above this goat as well. A third seal, also Assyrian, portrays the god Bel armed for combat against the demon Tiamat (Figure 14). Above Bel is the sun. Behind him are two unicorn goats, above which you find the crescent moon. Behind both the unicorn goats and Tiamat you find palm-trees. In all three, the unicorns' heads are always turned towards the tree, with the horn pointed at the tree (*Brown, 17*). Brown is convinced that this is all symbolic of the moon's journey from full to new and back again.

Figure 14. Merodach, or Bel, armed for the conflict with the dragon.

A skeptic would look at the unicorn goats in Figure 14 and conclude that the reason for the single horn is that the animal is in profile. If you examine another such relief, you can see that it was rather common to show two horns when the animal had two horns, even if shown in profile. Assyrian art tended to be very stylized, and the depiction of the elements didn't change much with the passage of time. The image in Figure 15 illustrates with a clean line drawing what the seal depicts when used.

A lovely rock relief found in Malatia (in Modern Armenia) shows the Assyrian gods in procession, which provides interesting insight into the Assyrian belief structure (Figure 16). In

Figure 15. Cylinder seal found in the Shara Temple.

the front is Ashur, the chief of the Assyrian pantheon, followed by Ishtar/Inanna, then Sin, En-lil, Shmash, Adad, and finally Ishtar of Arbela. Sin, the moon god, is standing upon a beast that could either be a bull or a unicorn. The original was excavated in the nineteenth century, but unfortunately most of the objects from this excavation were lost in a shipwreck or from looting the excavation site (*Place, 59*). Only an illustration of this relief survived.

Assyrian art is not the only place where we find the unicorn commonly represented with lunar symbols. A Phoenician gem found at Cnidos (modern day Turkey) shows the sun shining next to a large crescent moon above the heads of a unicorn bull and cow (*Brown, 18*). Unfortunately, Brown fails to consider that this may have been an object traded from Assyria, not native to Phoenicia, and doesn't provide any evidence to suggest one way or another through artistic style the cultural source of the carving on the gem.

Figure 16. Rock relief found in Malatia (in modern Armenia) showing the Assyrian gods in procession.

The Reality, Mythology, and Fantasies of Unicorns

Brown describes over twenty objects known to him through archaeological findings of Assyrian and Babylonian art showing the unicorn in the presence of the moon, a palm tree or trees, and often in opposition to the sun. Probably the most common representation of the unicorn in Mesopotamian art is the representation of a lion attacking a unicorn, sinking its teeth into its flank (*Brown, 23*).

While Brown claims that images of a unicorn were found by Heinrich Schliemann at Mycenae, Greece, on Cretan coins, and in early Egyptian paintings, following up on his sources I found that the image he sites by Schliemann at Mycenae was of two stags in profile, not unicorns. Both horns were clearly visible (*Schliemann, Figure 264*). Similarly one finds discrepancies in some of his other sources.

Brown may have depended upon people not validating his sources, and certainly the way his notes are formatted makes it difficult to actually track down his sources. However, most of the sources I was able to track down regarding Assyrian and Babylonian art do indeed show unicorns, lions, and trees, and these unicorns are, more often than not, associated with the moon.

Since the strongest link of the unicorn to mythology is in Assyria, it is worth considering what the moon meant to the Assyrians within their mythological framework, and with the Sumerians before them, as much of Assyrian myth borrowed heavily from the Sumerians. In ancient Sumer, the deity associated with the moon is Nanna/Suen/Asimbabbar (*Hall, 32*), the son of Enlil and Ninlil. When the Assyrians conquered Sumer, much like they associated Inanna with their Ishtar, they associated Nanna with their god Suen, often written in English as Sin, and over time the myths were blended. Suen was the father of Ishtar/Inanna and Erishkigal in both mythologies. During the period of 2600 through 2400 BCE, when Ur was the main seat of power in the region, Suen was considered the head of the pantheon, the father of gods, the creator of all things. The great ziggurat in Ur (modern Iraq), called E-gish-shir-gal, was raised to Suen.

Suen had a beard of lapis lazuli and rode on a winged bull. The bull, the crescent, and the tripod were his main symbols. You find shrines active in worship of Suen in Sumatra Harebesi in the Tektek mountains as late as the third century CE, and in Hadhramaut in south Arabia as late as the sixth century CE.

Sumerian ideas and culture continued to have a major influence through the fall of the old Babylonian kingdom in 1595 BCE, and in limited form in the religion of the region through the fall of the Neo-Babylonian empire in 539 CE. (*Hall, 4*). The polytheistic religion of Mesopotamia was adhered to in pockets through the eighteenth century CE, though large percentages of the population converted to Zoroastrianism, Christianity, and Islam. There continue to be many Jews living in the region, as well as those who identify with the other tribes of Israel.

It is good to pay close attention to Hall (*16*) when he cautions us that Sumerology is yet (by 1985, when his dissertation was published) in his opinion to reach the stage where it is possible to offer a definition of any symbol in Mesopotamian culture that will satisfy all scholars; and so Brown's speculations regarding the relationship of the unicorn to the god Nanna/Sin, made almost a century earlier, are problematic. To Hall, symbols are polysemous. In other words, they have multiple, if not an infinite number, of connotations (*Hall, 17*).

This ambiguity represents both the strength and the weakness of symbolic communication. Symbols, as they are transferred to other cultures through trade, often take on new meanings and sometimes lose their connections with the original meaning over both distance and time. Brown, with his limited resources, shows that the relationship between the moon and the unicorn survived in our symbolic language in both visual and literary art through the modern era, though I doubt much that Lewis Carroll, when he wrote of the fight between the unicorn and the lion in his *Alice Through the Looking Glass*, had the same meaning in mind as that intended by the ancient Sumerians in Ur.

Unlike with many of the ancient deities, we cannot infer anything from the meaning of two of the names associated with the moon god. In fact, the meaning of the deity's name may have been lost to the Sumerians and Assyrians. The Sumerian Gudea of Lagash wrote (in translation), "Suen, whose name no one can interpret" (*Hall, 41*).

While there is no known meaning of Nanna or Suen, there has been some success in identifying the meaning of Asimbabbar, which is relevant to this text. Asimbabbar roughly translates as wild ass (if you remember, this is exactly how the unicorn was described by Ctesias of Cnidus) who walks alone, or wild bull who walks alone. Hall (*42*) believes that the translation to bull makes more sense, due to the high frequency of association between the moon and the bull. Considering both how frequently the unicorn is described as a wild ass in ancient texts, and the solitary nature of the unicorn in ancient descriptions of the animal, as well as the common depiction of the unicorn with the moon in Assyrian art, Hall may be mis-translating this text. Unfortunately, we have no cuneiform that tells us what the Assyrians, or the Sumerians before them, named the creatures depicted in their art.

We do have an Assyrian name for a unicorn-like animal found on the black obelisk of Shalmaneser III. The cuneiform, when transliterated, gives us the word sakea. This animal could be a rhinoceros from India, depicted by someone who had never seen one, or a unicorn. The word would have to be found in the context of a more accurately depicted rhinoceros to settle the debate. With the horn squarely on the top of the head, I argue that sakea was the Assyrian word for unicorn.

Hall makes the deliberate choice to limit his investigation into Nanna/Suen/Asimbabbar to what is found in the surviving literature. He doesn't address the association of the unicorn with the moon in the Assyrian art, or anything in the archaeological or artistic record associated with either Sumer or Assyria. Of the three names, Asimbabbar was the least used in surviving Sumerian and Assyrian documentation, both in frequency, geography, and the timespan of surviving literature (*Hall, 54*).

Figure 17. Close-up of the Black Obelisk of Shalmaneser III.

In defense of Hall's translation, however, it must be noted that Suen is referred to as the "frisky calf of heaven" in many inscriptions (*Hall, 100*).

In the Sumerian religion, Nanna plays an important role as the god of the herds and provider of the prosperity of Ur (*Hall, 109*). Thus the noted association of Suen as the "frisky calf of heaven" is well within the context of Sumerian and probably Assyrian religions.

Hall does discuss the use of the crescent moon as a horn symbol. Apparently, most deities in Sumer and Assyria had double-horned or even four-horned crowns (*Hall, 134; Albenda, 173*). What is of interest and contradictory to Brown and Shepherd's theories is that the ancient Sumerians identified the moon with a lion, calling Nanna the "great lion of heaven and earth" (*Hall, 138*). While it is interesting that the Moon should be considered both prey (bull or wild ass?!) and predator (lion), there is nothing in Sumerian myth as we understand it that implies a conflict between these elements of the moon.

In fact, that both the lion and the unicorn (wild ass?) are appearing in Assyrian art together might be because they represent to the Assyrians, and the Sumerians before them, the many natures of the moon. We haven't to date found any literature that gives names to the unicorn-like images found in the Assyrian and Sumerian art. Perhaps the word "sakea" is the correct transliteration, but we don't know exactly what animal sakea was. It may have been wild ass, or something entirely different. Our understanding of the mythology of Sumer and Assyria, and their depictions of the unicorn, is limited by a lack of information that may never be able to end speculation.

In my readings of the surviving texts associated with either Ishtar/Inanna or Erishkigal, I have learned nothing of unicorns or the wild ass. Both Erishkigal and Ishtar/Inanna were married to spouses nicknamed "bull." Erishkigal was married to Gugalanna, the bull of heaven. Inanna was married to Dumuzi, whom she calls a wild bull in the sensual poem *The Courtship of Inanna and Dumuzi* (*Wolkstein, Kramer, 36–37*). Inanna does, however, make an interesting comment about a single horn in the same poem. She says, "What I tell you, let the singer weave into song, what I tell you, let it flow from ear to mouth, let it pass from old to young: my vulva, the horn, the boat of Heaven, is full of eagerness like the young moon."

The Reality, Mythology, and Fantasies of Unicorns

The horn. Not multiple horns, a single horn. Is it possible that the symbol represented by the single horn of the unicorn is Inanna's vulva, or more specifically her clitoris? Is it possible that the beast that was the medieval symbol of virginity and chastity is a symbol for the vulva of the Sumerian goddess of love and war? The very goddess who stole from Enki, the Sumerian god of wisdom, the art of love-making, the art of kissing the phallus, and the art of prostitution (*Wolkstein, Kramer, 17*). It is possible, but surprising.

Inanna became one of the most popular deities of ancient Mesopotamia, adopted by many cultures with an active cult through the eighteenth century CE (*Parpola, 17*). Undertaking a study into this would be worth at least one Ph.D. dissertation. To my knowledge, there is little literature associated with Erishkigal other than the myths depicting Inanna's descent into the underworld and Erishkigal's marriage to Nergal, and Erishkigal as one of the recipients of gifts in the Sumerian poem, *The Death of Ur-Namma*. There is only one known possible depiction of Erishkigal in art (Figure 13), a large terracotta plaque whose authenticity is under dispute (*Albenda*).

The primary argument against the plaque being authentic is that it is a more realistic depiction of the female form than otherwise found in Mesopotamian art of the period. However, the clay of the plaque was tested in two locations and found to have been fired between 2000 and 3700 years ago. (*Albenda, 171*). I frankly think that dismissing the plaque on the basis of artistic and stylistic issues is a fallacious argument. The more you become acquainted with the art found by Sir Leonard Wooley in Ur in the 1920s, the more you can appreciate the skill of the ancient Sumerian artists. I can certainly appreciate Albenda's concerns regarding the lack of provenance for the plaque, but this is far from a unique issue in antiquities.

There is nothing in this plaque (Figure 13) to indicate whether Erishkigal (if this is Erishkigal) has any association with unicorns. The figure rests her taloned claws on the backs of two lions. We commonly find depictions of Inanna (and later Ishtar) associated with lions. I presented the archaeological evidence associating Inanna/Ishtar with unicorns in a prior chapter, so I'm not going to reiterate that here other than to say that it is absurd to look at ancient cultures and expect more consistency in belief than in our own culture. While the textual evidence doesn't support the association of the moon god with unicorns, the artistic evidence at least supports the moon god's daughter as having something to do with unicorns.

There is another relief (Figure 18) we should consider. This one has been identified as Ishtar, and was made in the second century BCE. This relief shows a winged naked goddess; but instead of owls and lions, this one has two unicorn goats. Currently housed in the Louvre, this relief is not as well-preserved as the

Figure 18. Terracotta relief of Ishtar with wings from Larsa.

one with the owls commonly associated with Erishkigal, but is similar in workmanship. In my opinion, the existence of Figure 18 should put Albenda's concerns to rest. It may provide the clearest visual link between the Ishtar cult and unicorns.

A second part of Brown's thesis is that the tree in Assyrian art represents the sacred grove, the gateway to the underworld. It is worth examining what modern scholarship has to say on the motif of the Sacred Tree in Sumerian and Assyrian art. Giovino examines the history of the various theses of the role, if any, of the Sacred Tree as a cult object. One of the things that must be understood about the tree is that it is frequently depicted as banded, and various translations of the text that refers to the Sacred Tree describe it as banded. Interestingly enough, both furniture legs and architectural columns found in Assyrian archaeological sites were also wrapped by metal bands in the same way the images show the bands on the Sacred Tree (*Giovino, 161*).

The poles found outside a temple to the moon god Sin resemble trees. Apparently, they were used in the Assyrian New Year's festival (*Giovino, 161*), which we already know included a unicorn paraded upon a pole as part of the celebration (*Parpola, 438*). Thus, indirectly, we have a correlation between Brown's notion connecting the unicorn to the Assyrian moon god and the sacred tree through the Assyrian New Year's.

Bunt (*434*) makes the argument that rather than the strife between the unicorn and the lion being represented by the daily cycle of the moon and the sun, or the solar eclipse, that it represents the changing of the seasons. He posits that since the summer solstice occurs when Leo is ascendant in the sky, since the summer in Mesopotamia was a season of death, and since spring begins when Taurus is ascendant, that the conflict between the lion and the unicorn represents transition from spring to summer.

Considering that the parade of the gods occurs at the new year, or the rise of Taurus in the spring, it is possible that Bunt is onto something, and that after all this, it is a bull we're seeing, not a unicorn, in the art of Sumer and Assyria. Since Bunt wrote his theories, we've learned a lot more about the development of astrology in Mesopotamia. The twelve signs of the zodiac that we've become familiar with, along with some signs that weren't picked up by the Greeks (serpent, crow, eagle, and fish), were not developed in Mesopotamia until rather late in antiquity (*Rogers, 9*).

While it was common to find the lion and unicorn in combat in the context of the symbols for the sun, moon, and Venus (Ishtar/Inanna), there is a magnificent cylinder seal that shows what could have been the constellations as they were understood by the Sumerians (Figure 19). As you can see when you look on it, there is little to match the twelve signs of the zodiac (*Rogers, 10*). Unfortunately, Bunt's theory is not consistent with the evidence at hand.

To help understand all of this a bit better, it is worthwhile to look into the literature of the ancient Sumer. The Sumerian version of the epic poem *Gilgamesh* (called "Gilgames" in Sumerian) begins with Inanna weeping over a tree that she had planted herself and nursed for ten years. Now she longs to turn its wood into a bed and a chair, but the tree is haunted by a dark maid named Lilith, who dwells in the trunk, and a snake immune to her incantations, which dwells in its roots. Inanna asks Gilgames to help her, which he does, uprooting the tree, driving away Lilith, who flees into the wilderness, and killing the snake. He gives Inanna the wood for her bed and chair, taking only the roots and some branches for himself, from which he fashions a ball and a mallet (*Gilgames, lines 123–165*). This mallet unfortunately falls into the underworld, and Gilgames's servant Enkidu vows to travel into the underworld to retrieve it for Gilgames. His failure to return from the underworld after he disregards Gilgames's instructions on how to enter the underworld clandestinely, is the catalyst which begins Gilgames's mythic journey.

Figure 19. Cylinder seal impression from the Elamite capital of Susa.

This older form of the story not only has Gilgames helping Inanna, instead of defying her, but also involves a tree precious to her. It is worth remembering that the New Year's celebration in Sumer and Assyria was also a celebration of Inanna, and that she is the daughter of the moon. The nature of the tree, however, is not what Brown expected. It is not at the gateway to the underworld. The loss of the mallet formed from its wood begins a quest that involves both entry into the underworld and the heart-wrenching loss associated with Enkidu's failure to return.

The symbolic nature of the unicorn in the context of all of this remains a mystery, as none of the surviving texts describe the unicorn's role in the new year's parade, and the fact that it had a role at all is only understood from the archaeological records. Black and Green (*156*), in their illustrated dictionary *Gods, Demons and Symbols of Ancient Mesopotamia*, classify the image that so many have described as a unicorn bull as just cattle. Unfortunately, Black and Green do not provide any context for this categorization. As for myself, I remain convinced that when the artisans of ancient Mesopotamia wanted to depict an animal that had two horns, they etched a second horn onto the animal, and that the depiction of a single horn is a deliberate choice.

As for the parade itself, we only have fragments of an understanding of it. We know that there was a parade associated with the new year in the Babylonian era, from the myth of how the Babylonian god Marduk fought Tiamat, a cosmological dragon. The parade consisted of the gods of Babylonia escorting Marduk to battle for them. The festival was celebrated at the sowing of barley, in late March or early April, on the first day of the Babylonian year.

There is very little of the Sumerian version of the myth of the gods' battle with the dragon that reached us, despite there being three versions of the Sumerian telling of the myth. The first telling comes from the Sumerian version of the epic *Gilgames*. The Sumerian water god Enki goes into battle with the Kur, a beast with the same name as the Sumerian underworld, to rescue the moon god's other daughter, Erishkigal. She had been abducted by the Kur and taken to the underworld. Enki sailed out on his boat and attacked the Kur with all kinds of stones. The Kur fought back with the primal waters (*Kramer, Location 2182*).

We have no account of his victory, but through a different myth, that of Inanna's descent into the underworld, we know that Erishkigal not only remained in the underworld, but ruled there as queen, likely put in that role by Enki.

The second version of the story is the epic known to us as *The Feats and Exploits of Ninurta*. Like the tale of Enki, this story is not completely known due to a combination of untranslatable text and missing passages from the broken tablets that the scribes etched the story onto over five thousand years ago. In this version, Ninurta, the warrior god and son of Enlil, is sent to destroy the Kur for some unknown reason and succeeds; but because of this the land is flooded with primeval waters, and no fresh water can reach the fields and gardens. There is famine in the land. Ninurta then builds a wall on top of the Kur, which allows the normal flow of waters, and prosperity returns to the lands (*Kramer, Location 2243*).

The third version, *Inanna and Ebih*, involves Inanna who destroys the mountain Ebih, which is identified with the Kur. Upon its defeat, she then stands upon it in triumph.

The impression from a Sumerian calendar seal in Figure 20 shows what appears to be the goddess Inanna, armed for war, on a mountain top from which grows a desolate tree. The water god Enki, with flowing streams of water and fish, is stepping over what appears to be a unicorn. You also see Utu, with his saw knife and fiery rays, rising from the underworld, though he also holds a mace or a mallet. Perhaps it is Enkidu retrieving the mallet for Gilgames as promised, and it is possible that the figure on the far left with the bow is Gilgames, and behind him

Figure 20. Sumerian seal showing Inanna, Utu, and Enki.

is a lion. The lone figure which doesn't fit in with the Gilgames interpretation is the one on the far right: the Sumerian god Isimud, Enki's messenger. Isimud figures in a different story, in which Inanna gets Enki drunk and steals the "Me," divine powers, from him. That story does not involve any of the other personages believed to be in this image.

Kramer believes that the figure rising from the underworld is Utu, the Sumerian sun god, due mostly to the saw knife he holds, but I agree with Kramer that here we find many of the actors of that part of the Sumerian version of the Gilgames epic known to us as *Gilgames, Enkidu, and the Netherworld* (*Kramer, Location 1891 of 3609*).

Lavers (*229–233*) also noticed the unicorn on that Sumerian seal and the potential link to the Gilgames epic. In his case, he explores the Assyrian version of the story despite the seal being a Sumerian seal, where Enkidu is depicted as a wild man who eats grass and is civilized by a harlot who seduces him. Likely the harlot would have been in the service of Ishtar, as there are indications that the cult of Ishtar had divine harlots. Lavers noticed the parallel to how unicorns are also captured by women and thus become tame, and wondered if in earlier versions of the story Enkidu might have had a horn. Unfortunately, we know that in the Sumerian version of the epic, not only didn't Enkidu have a horn, he was not a wild man seduced into civilization by a woman; he was Gilgames's loyal but disobedient servant.

Cryptically, the unicorn and the lion sit mysteriously within a seal, abstractly depicting what was perhaps the greatest myth that has come from Sumer. As neither figure is in the surviving text we have of the myth itself, we don't know why the artist who created the seal depicting this myth felt it important to include these symbolic creatures along with their hero and three deities.

There is one more tantalizing link between the lion and the unicorn to be found in ancient Sumer. In the excavation of Ur between 1922 and 1934, Sir Leonard Woolley found five game boards of what is now known of as the Royal Game of Ur. All five game boards were substantively identical though made from different materials and with different decorations. Bunt (*Antiquity, 425*) observes that one of the boards depicts the lion and the unicorn in opposition in the game itself. Also of note is that on the most ancient versions of the board you find the rosette symbol associated with the goddess Inanna.

They found instructions on how to play this game. It is an exciting game of chase, which was played in multiple cultures across many centuries. It is important to note two things regarding the play of the game. The first is that over time landing in certain squares took on a predictive nature, the other is that people used to bet on the outcomes.

The version of the board depicted in Figure 21, while incomplete, shows bulls, goats, at least one unicorn, and a lion.

There is one final myth worth mentioning that involves both a unicorn and a lion. A manuscript from the Coptic Church, written about 600 CE, portrays the crucifixion and death of Jesus of Nazareth and his descent into Hell, which he'll destroy. This particular manuscript describes how, after Jesus dies, he takes a cup of water, speaks a prayer over it, blessing it with the Hebrew name of his Father, Iaō Sabaōth, and then pours it into the sea. The sea parts to reveal a golden field at the bottom where a unicorn lies. The unicorn seems surprised to see Jesus and asks, "Who are you who stands here and thus, in the body, yea, in the flesh, who has not been given into my hands?"

Figure 21. The game of Ur.

Jesus replies, "I am Israēl Ēl, the force of Iaō Sabaōth, the great power of Barbaraōth." The unicorn becomes terrified of this and flees. (*Coptic Magical Papyri, 26th April 2019*)

The Christian story of the harrowing of Hell is a common one throughout the ancient and medieval worlds, persisting through Dante's Inferno and other Catholic and Orthodox stories. This, however, is unique in the role of the unicorn in the story. In other Coptic accounts of Jesus's death, Abaddon, the angel of death is confused when Jesus's soul doesn't appear in hell after he dies. He goes there to find Jesus still in the tomb, laughing at him. The unicorn has the same role as death, terrified that he has no power over Jesus.

It helps to remember that the Greek translation of Psalm 21 (Psalm 22 in most Western Bibles) is quoted by Jesus as he is dying, "My God, my God, why have you forsaken me?" The Greek and Coptic translations of the sixth century CE translates what follows as, "Rescue my soul from the sword, and from a dog's claw my only life! Save me from a lion's mouth, and my lowliness from the horns of unicorns!" (*NETS translation of the Septuagint*).

Albrecht Dürer's *Ritter, Tod und Teufel* (Figure 22) depicts a knight riding with his dog menaced by both death and the devil. His drawing uncharacteristically depicts the devil with a single horn. Christians of the sixth century CE would have had experience with the still existing cults associated with both Ishtar/Inanna and Erishkigal, and the various Mesopotamian kingdoms and religions are frequently referred to in Judaic and Christian scripture as a representation of evil in the world. If the unicorn was associated with Erishkigal or with Ishtar/Inanna, it would not be surprising that, in the sixth century CE, some Christians would have identified the unicorn with both hell and evil. If anything, that identification might be a good indication that the unicorn is mythologically linked to Erishkigal.

Unless future archaeological excavations reveal myths or rituals as yet undiscovered, the role of the unicorn within Sumer may never be known. More importantly, we may never truly understand the nature of the relationship between the lion and the unicorn, sometimes depicted as antagonistic, sometimes as peaceable. Regardless, the victory of the lion over the unicorn is as uncertain as anything else about the unicorn.

Figure 22. Albrecht Dürer's *Ritter, Tod und Teufel*.

THE MYTH OF THE UNICORN HUNT

Pliny the Elder wrote of the unicorn, "This animal, they say, cannot be taken alive" (*Shepherd, 37*).

And yet, much of medieval lore and historical writing about the unicorn across all of the cultures I could find had legends on how and why to hunt this most dangerous of beasts. There are two kinds of hunts: the physical hunt, trying to bring down a dangerous, large, and powerful animal; and the spiritual hunt. Despite all of the descriptions of the unicorn that came down from the ancients, medieval European imagination was instead inspired by various bestiaries, most of which were condemned by the Church as nonsense or even as heresy.

With that in mind, there are two questions to ask: how to hunt a unicorn, and why. Those questions are somewhat entwined, and culturally dependent. We'll start in Europe, where both the how and the why are somewhat infamous and very odd.

A particular bestiary was extremely influential in Western Europe for over a thousand years despite being condemned by Pope Gelasius as a work of heretics. The bestiary, *Physiologus*, describes the unicorn as a small animal, like a goat kid, rather fierce, with a single horn on its head. The *Physiologus* claims no hunter can capture this beast by force, but if a virgin waits in an area where the unicorn lives, it will come to her and place its head on her lap. If she pets it, it may fall asleep and thus be captured. The ancient commentary on Saint Basil's *Hexaemeron* tells much the same story and may be the source of the myth that you hunt a unicorn with a virgin as bait (*Shepherd, 45–51*).

The unknown author wrote, "In Deuteronomy Moses said while blessing Joseph, 'His beauty is that of the firstling bull, and his horns are the horns of the unicorn' (*Deut. 33:17*). The Monoceros, that is, the unicorn, has this nature: he is a small animal like the kid, is exceedingly shrewd, and has one horn in the middle of his head. The hunter cannot approach him because he is extremely strong. How then do they hunt the beast? Hunters place a chaste virgin before him. He bounds forth into her lap and she warms and nourishes the animal and takes him into the palace of the kings." (*Shepherd, 45–51*).

This bestiary was a medieval bestseller. The only book more widely distributed and read was the Bible. Many copies were illustrated, increasing people's delight in the volume, which frequently skipped from descriptions of animals and fantasies into the allegorical material that many medieval Europeans loved.

The unknown author continues, "The unicorn has one horn because the Savior said, 'I and the Father are one' (*John 10:30*). 'For he has raised up a horn of salvation for us in the house of his servant David' (*Luke 1:69*). Coming down from heaven, he came into the womb of the Virgin Mary. 'He was loved like the son of the unicorns' (*Psalm 22:21*) as David said in the psalm." Also, "The unicorn is like the kid, as is our Savior according to the Apostle: 'He was made in the likeness of sinful flesh and for sin he condemned sin in the flesh' (*Romans 8:3*). This was spoken well of the unicorn." (*Shepherd, 45–51*).

The wide distribution and common knowledge of this description of the unicorn well explains why Marco Polo was so shocked to behold an actual unicorn, both larger and uglier than the *Physiologus* had led him to expect.

This myth did the medieval equivalent of going viral. To the medieval European Christians, the story of a ferocious beast tamed by a virgin appeared as an apt metaphor for demonic creatures tamed by Virgin Mary. Hildegard of Bingen—an amazing author, composer, mystic, pharmacist, poet, theologian, and abbess—expounded about the use of the virgin in hunting a unicorn. She writes:

"The unicorn is more hot than cold. Its strength is greater than its heat. It eats clean plants. In moving it has a leap, and it flees humans and other animals, except those that are of its kind, and so it cannot be captured. It especially fears a man, and shuns him. Just as the serpent in the first fall shunned the man and got to know the woman, so this animal avoids a man but follows a woman. There was a certain philosopher who scrutinized the nature of animals, and he marveled greatly that capturing this animal, by any skill, was impossible. One day he went hunting, as he usually did, and was accompanied by men, women, and girls. The girls walked separately from the others, and played among the flowers. Seeing the girls, a unicorn shortened its leaps and gradually drew near. It sat on its hind legs, diligently gazing at them from afar. The philosopher, seeing this, thought hard about it; he understood that a unicorn could be captured by girls. A unicorn, seeing a girl from afar, wonders that she has no beard but does have the shape of a person. If two or three girls are together, it is more amazed, and is caught more quickly when its eyes are fixed on them. The girls by whose means the unicorn is captured must be nobles, not country girls. They should be neither completely grown nor entirely small, but in the midst of adolescence. The unicorn loves them, because it knows that they are gentle and sweet." (*Bingen, 210*).

Her text was more than just a bestiary, as it offered up cures for various ills, and it was widely read and valued. The unicorn, according to Hildegard of Bingen, got its healing power from an annual trip to the land that contains the waters of paradise, where it eats from the plants that grow there. Its liver would cure leprosy. Its skin would prevent disease and fever. The hoof of the unicorn she credited with detecting poison.

The oddest thing in her text is that no magical properties are to be found in the unicorn's horn. We'll explore the horn and its presumptive magical properties in a later chapter, but between the horn, the hoof, the skin, and the liver, there were many practical reasons for hunting the unicorn.

There are also spiritual reasons. If we take a fresh look at the *Physiologus*, there are some sections I didn't quote. Those sections concern themselves with the unicorn as a living analogy to the incarnation of God in the person of Jesus of Nazareth, as believed within Christianity. The anonymous author writes, "He (the unicorn) is said to be shrewd since neither principalities, powers, thrones, nor dominations can comprehend him, nor can hell hold him. He is small because of the humility of his incarnation." Later, in the same paragraph, "The unicorn is like the kid, as is our Savior, according to the Apostle: 'He was made in the likeness of sinful flesh and for sin he condemned sin in the flesh' (*Romans 8:3*). This was spoken well of the unicorn" (*Physiologus*). The hunt for the unicorn is the hunt for God within the world.

There are two interesting variations of the *Physiologus*. The Provençal version compares the unicorn to the Devil, not to an incarnation of God, and proposes that the reason the virgin is the only one to overcome the unicorn is because evil can only be overcome by virtue. The other interesting variation, the Syriac version, states, "There is an animal called dagga, extremely gentle, which the hunters are unable to capture because of its great strength. It has in the middle of its brow a single horn. But observe the ruse by which the huntsmen take it. They lead forth a young virgin, pure and chaste, to whom, when the animal sees her, he approaches, throwing himself upon her. Then the girl offers him her breasts, and the animal begins to suck the breasts of the maiden and to conduct himself familiarly with her. Then the girl, while sitting quietly, reaches forth her hand and grasps the horn on the animal's brow, and at this point the huntsmen come up and take the beast and go away with him to the king." (*Shepherd, 49*).

The Syriac version of the *Physiologus* avoids reference to allegorical symbolism of later versions. The Syriac version of the unicorn hunt is the oldest version we have of this story in the west. In this version, the actions of the girl reflect a different and equally powerful allegory of the complexities of human sexuality.

Other medieval authors, in describing the unicorn hunt, would require that the maiden be naked, and that if the girl was not a virgin but pretended to be one, the unicorn would naturally kill the pretender. Some wrote that the virgin must be bound to a tree, so that the unicorn would know her to be completely harmless.

The reason for the link between the virgin and the unicorn being tied to medieval Christian allegory of the life of Jesus comes from teachings that Jesus's mother, Mary, was a virgin when she conceived and bore him. Many believe that this is the symbolic language represented in the famous Unicorn

Figure 23. Statue of girl with unicorn from Vigeland Park in Oslo.

Tapestries now housed in the Cloisters in New York City, a branch of the Metropolitan Museum of Art. In these tapestries, the unicorn is hunted much like a stag, and killed while defending itself. Famously, the last tapestry of the series shows the unicorn as no longer dead. There are two fragments of tapestries in the collection, one of which shows the unicorn with a woman, who may be the required virgin in the medieval European edition of the unicorn hunt narrative.

In the hunting and slaying of the unicorn (Jesus), the medieval Christians saw themselves as active participants in the death of Jesus. By driving the unicorn to its death, they also brought about the death of Jesus. The story does not end with the death but continues with his resurrection and assumption into heaven. While on the cross and suffering, the belief that Jesus forgives those who killed him is a core part of the hope Christians have for themselves. In their identification with those who kill Jesus, they recognize that their sins are not better than the sins of those who actually killed him. Christians ritualize their identification with those who kill Jesus two times during their ritual cycle. The first is on Palm Sunday, often called Passion Sunday, and the second is on Good Friday. It is not surprising that to the medieval Christians the unicorn represents Jesus. They who hunt the unicorn are they who killed the Son of God.

The Reality, Mythology, and Fantasies of Unicorns

Figure 24. The unicorn reborn.

Later forms of this story elaborate the hunt of the unicorn in rather odd ways. A king had two sons, one who killed himself and one who was so horribly hurt that the only remedy was the blood of a unicorn. The king sought the most beautiful woman in his kingdom and sat her with six maiden attendants in his garden.

There they waited for the unicorn, while hunters with dogs drove the unicorn to the maiden (*Shepard, 58*).

In this version, the maiden is the refuge for a unicorn frightened from hunters and dogs. The dogs are traditionally named Mercy, Truth, Justice, and Peace, formerly foes, but unified in their shared hunt for the unicorn. Once the unicorn is caught, its blood is used to cure the son who is hurt. Symbolically, the father is God, the first son is equated in the story to Satan, the second to Adam, and the unicorn again is Jesus, whose blood is the salvation not only for Adam, but for all of humanity (*Shepard, 59*).

It was not uncommon to paint the unicorn hunt with the unicorn being driven by the hunters to a particular virgin, Mary. The painting in Figure 25 is one example of many that illustrate the unicorn hunt as part of the Annunciation of Mary.

Associating the unicorn hunt with the annunciation, or the announcement to Mary by the angels that she is to become pregnant with God's child, is a rather particular twist on the myth which started rather sexually in the original tellings. Depictions of the unicorn as part of the story of the annunciation were halted by the Council of Trent in 1563 (*Beer, 103*).

Figure 25. The Annunciation as an Allegorical Unicorn Hunt.

THE REALITY, MYTHOLOGY, AND FANTASIES OF UNICORNS

Like that of medieval Europe, much of the writing of the Islamic world on the nature of the unicorn is concerned with its morphology and biology. The stories that tell of hunting the karkadan are not, however, mythological in nature. There is no allegorical significance to the slaying of this beast, and nothing holy about hunting it.

That doesn't mean that we don't find the virgin irrelevant to stories of hunting the unicorn in Arabic tales. In the fourteenth century, Al Damiri writes that if you place a virgin or a beautiful girl in the path of a unicorn, as soon as he sees her, he will leap into her lap, making signs he wishes to drink her milk. After he has suckled, he lies down drunk and thus is captured by the hunters (*Ettinghausen, 62*).

Most stories written of the hunt for a unicorn which come from Islamic literature are the stories of a bold hero such as the hero of the *Shah-namah*. In the *Shah-namah*, Gushtap is sent to hunt and kill a unicorn during his exile in Rûm by Caesar. His son, Isfandiyar, must kill two karkadan as two of the seven feats he must perform to free his sisters. The third hero of the *Shah-namah*, Iskandar, encounters an entire herd of the karkadan and slays their leader. The fourth hero of the *Shah-namah* to slay the karkadan does so while in disguise in the court of Shangul of India. Each of these heroes will next tackle a dragon.

In some Islamic stories, the karkadan is not tamed by virginity, but by music. The karkadan would stop and listen to bird song, to organs, and other musical instruments. Another who might tame this ferocious beast is a lovesick poet. An important difference between Islamic lore of the unicorn as compared to that of other traditions is that the karkadan represents a powerful and tyrannical king. The beast is evil and only kings of great power, such as Suleiman, can pacify it. Only a great hero can kill it (*Ettinghausen*).

In China, no hero or hunter ever killed a qilin, though one was wounded by a hunter just before the death of Confucius. However, the qilin is a sacred beast, thought to descend from Heaven, refusing to tread on any living thing, including insects or blades of grass.

In the so-called age of exploration, European explorers roamed areas of the world long unknown to them. They also hunted for the unicorn in their explorations.

Lavers contributes to our understanding of those who hunted for the unicorn by following those European explorers who traveled the globe. No longer was a virgin necessary in the hunt; one simply needed to travel. As I mentioned in an earlier chapter, the first explorer to report the finding of a unicorn in his travels was Captain Samuel Turner in his journey through Tibet. In his *Account of an Embassy to the Court of the Teshoo Lama in Tibet*, written in 1800, he writes:

> "He had a very curious creature, he (the Rajah) told me, then in his possession; a sort of horse, with a horn growing from the middle of its forehead. He had once another of the same species; but it died. I could not discover from whence it came, or obtain any other explanation other than 'burra dûre!' ('a great way off!'). I expressed a very earnest desire to see a creature so curious and uncommon, and told him that we had representations of an animal called a unicorn, to which his description answered; but it was generally considered as fabulous. He again assured me of the truth of what he had told me, and promised I should see it; but I never had sight of it." (*Lavers*, 156).

Turner wasn't the only British military man to be told of unicorns in Tibet. I have already mentioned that Major Latter had joined the hunt to find a unicorn. He took the subject seriously and published his account in the *Quarterly Journal (1821)*. He wrote:

> "In a Thibetan (a spelling variant) manuscript which I procured the other day from the hills, the unicorn is classed under the head of those animals whose hooves are divided; it is called the one-horned tso'po. Upon inquiring what kind of animal it was, to our astonishment the person who brought me the manuscript described exactly the unicorn of ancients, saying that it was a native of the interior of Thibet, fierce, and extremely wild, seldom if ever caught alive. They go together in herds like our wild buffaloes, and are very frequently met with on the borders of the great desert about a month's journey from Lassa, in that part of the country inhabited by wandering Tartars."

French missionaries Evariste Huc and Joseph Gabe traveled to Tibet and entered the forbidden city of Lhasa in 1846. Huc wrote about the Tibetan unicorn's horn in his account of the journey. "A horn of this animal (tsopo) was fifty centimeters in length and twelve centimeters in circumference from the root; it grew smaller and smaller and terminated in a point. It was almost straight, black, and somewhat flat at the sides. It had fifteen rings, but they were only prominent on one side" (*Lavers, 159*).

Tibet wasn't the only place the European explorers turned to in their hopes of finding a unicorn. In 1783, the Swedish naturalist Anders Sparrman cited the account of many South Africans that unicorns were common near the Cape of Good Hope (*Lavers, 160*). Baron Friedrich von Wurmb reported being told by a number of individuals of a "one horn'd" beast that looks like a horse with divided hoofs. He ordered them to bring him one, alive or dead, but none were ever brought (*Lavers, 161*).

In 1838, Albrecht Von Katte was told by Ethiopian soldiers that unicorns lived in central Africa. There are two items of import in his account.

> "It is true that their reports are not entirely consistent, but neither are they contradictory. Those who assert that they have seen the animal give the same description of it that Pliny left us. They say, that is, that it has the hoofs of the horse and the same shape as a horse, that it is grey in color and has a strong horn in the middle of its brow... They say also that it is very shy and therefore hard to approach. These people find great likeness between it and the unicorn shown on the English arms, but when I showed them a picture of the rhinoceros they said at once: 'that is not it; that is another animal'." (*Lavers, 163*).

Philip Henry Gosse FRS collected a number of such accounts, which he placed into his 1861 book *The Romance of Natural History*. On the basis of this book, the British governor of Uganda set out in 1899 on what turned out to be the last funded hunt for the unicorn, at least by the European colonial powers. Undertaken partially to help return six pigmies to their home, the Governor hoped to spot a unicorn. Along the way, he learned of a beast called an atti by his Pigmy guides, or as an okapi by the Mbuba. Western scholarship has adopted okapi as the scientific name for the species. The okapi have cloven feet and a hide with distinctive coloring. The forehead of the okapi is described as deep red chestnut; neck, shoulders, and torso range in tone from black to red. The belly is black, except at the knees. The hindquarters are snowy white, marked with purple-black stripes (*Lavers, 187*).

This animal was known to the ancients. There is a panel in Persepolis showing an okapi being taken to King Xerces, but its existence hadn't been known to the more contemporary Europeans. In their excitement at the find of this unique animal, a distant relative of the giraffe, they forgot about continuing their hunt for the unicorn (*Lavers, 195*).

Satyajit Ray's delightful fictional story *The Unicorn Expedition* tells of explorers hunting for unicorns. The hunters in this story aren't aiming to slay a unicorn but merely to find if the beast actually lives in Tibet, as they've learned. The story begins with the last entry of the diary of a husband who recently passed on, addressed to his widow, which says, "I saw a herd of unicorns today. I write this in the full possession of my senses" (*Ray, 156*).

I must confess that if I came into the possession of just such a diary, I too would journey to the Himalayas in the hopes of seeing just such a herd.

THE MYTHOLOGY OF THE UNICORN'S HORN

Odel Shepherd, from whose immortal writing stems much of a modern understanding of unicorn lore, decided that writing "the horn of the unicorn" was a tedious thing to do. He coined the term alicorn to refer to the horn of the unicorn. Hildegard of Bingen may have believed that there was nothing special about the alicorn. To the rest of medieval Europe, the horn was a good part of what made the unicorn so precious.

There is an old version of the *Physiologus*, written in Greek, which provides an example of supposed properties of an alicorn: that it purifies what it touches. In this translation, the unicorn makes the sign of a cross over the water using its horn, and poison in the water is immediately rendered harmless (*Shepard, 73*).

The poet Natalis Comes, who mostly wrote about using myth as an allegorical way to understand humans and their nature, described the curative properties of an alicorn in a poem he wrote about hunting.

> Far on the edge of the world and beyond the banks of the Ganges,
> Savage and lone, is a place in the realm of the King of the Hindus.
> Where there is born a beast as large as a stag in stature,
> Dark on the back, solid-hoofed, very fierce, and shaped like a bullock.
> Mighty and black is the horn that springs from the animal's forehead,

Terrible unto his foe, a defense and a weapon of onslaught.
Often the poisoners steal to the banks of that swift-flowing river,
Fouling the waves with disease by their secret insidious poisons;
After them comes this beast and dips his horn in the water,
Cleansing the venom away and leaving the stream to flow purely
So that the forest-dwellers may drink once more by the margin.
Also men say that the beast delights in the embrace of a virgin,
Falling asleep in her arms and taking sweet rest on her bosom.
Ah! but, awaking, he finds he is bound by ropes and by shackles.
Strange is the tale, indeed, yet so, they say, he is taken,
Whether it be that the seeds of love have been sown by great Nature
Deep in his blood or for some more hidden mysterious reason.
(*Shepherd, 61*)

Obviously, the poem builds on the tradition of the unicorn as a symbol for Christ, who makes the world and its sins pure through his sacrifice on the cross. However, it was the ability to transform a poisoned substance into something safe to eat or drink that fired the imaginations of the aristocracy, who all too often had to worry about being poisoned. This is the reason why the narwhal's tooth became such a precious item, treasured by royalty and enriching merchants and fishermen who took full advantage of the gullibility of the nobles.

What I find fascinating about the poem is that it not only places the unicorn in India, but near to the Ganges, where Marco Polo beheld a unicorn in the later thirteenth century. Of course, the one-horned rhinoceros is also found along the banks of the Ganges.

The idea that the unicorn could purify water became a common motif in art, as well as one of the many uses to which the alicorn was put.

The Garden of Earthly Delights by Hieronymus Bosch (Figure 26) has one of many representations of the unicorn putting its horn into water so that both itself and other animals might safely drink.

The horn was frequently described as black in classical Greek and Roman sources, despite the fact that the narwhal's tooth, being white, was commonly thought to be the horn of a unicorn. Various scholars described the alicorn at varying lengths, anywhere from Ctesias who proclaimed it a cubit in length (equal to ~44 cm or ~18 inches) to Albertus Magnus who described it as ten feet in length. Albertus Magnus was

Figure 26. Fragment from Hieronymus Bosch's *Garden of Earthly Delights.*

both a noted naturalist, who made extensive study of animals, and a respected scientist of his era; so we can only assume that he had observed a long narwhal tusk, which can grow to be as long as 3.1 meters, or approximately ten feet.

The discrepancy between the narwhal tusk and the literary descriptions of an alicorn did distress at least one Renaissance scholar. Andrea Bacci had noted this in his analysis of the works of Aelian and Pliny, but was loath to declare that the specimen owned by his patron, Don Francesco di Medici, was anything other than a genuine alicorn (*Shephard, 162*).

Throughout history, many depictions, especially those in European art, show the alicorn to grow in either rings or spirals, such as the tusk of a narwhal. The depictions of the alicorn, both in the Persepolis bas reliefs and in the Indus Valley seals, show the alicorn as curved. If you look closely at the horn in some of the relief sculptures, you can see that originally they were meant to depict the horn as having either rings or spirals, but the detailing has been worn away by time.

Arab literature regarding the horn of the unicorn is rather fanciful in a rather different way. According to both Al Dimari and Algiahid, when the alicorn is cut open, you will find the figures of men, birds, animals, and certain kinds of trees inside.

The Reality, Mythology, and Fantasies of Unicorns

I suspect the authors had seen carved elephant tusks and thought them to be unicorn horns. Other Arab authors claim that the horn emits music as the unicorn moves about, through perforations in the horn itself.

Because of the presumed property of purifying food and drink of poisons, fake alicorns were quite a cottage industry, and "real" alicorns were precious and treasured. Another cottage industry that arose was a litany of tests to tell the real from the fake. It is amusing to think that, much like with the efforts to turn lead into gold, the roots of the scientific method are founded in discerning fake alicorns from "real" alicorns.

David de Pomis, a Jewish physician and philosopher of the sixteenth century, wrote:

> "The unicorn is a beast that has one horn in its brow, and this horn is good against poison and pestilential fevers. But one is to observe that there is very little of the true horn to be found, most of that which is sold as such being either stag's horn or elephant's tusk. The common test which consists in placing the object in water to see whether bubbles will rise is not at all to be trusted, and therefore, wishing to benefit the world and to expose the wicked persons who sell worthless things at great prices, I take

Figure 27. Relief of a lion and unicorn from Persepolis.

Figure 28. Page from Pierre Pomet's *History Générale des drogues*.

this occasion to describe a true test by which one may know the genuine horn from the false. The test is this: place the horn in a vessel of any sort of material you like, and with it three or four live and large scorpions, keeping the vessel covered. If you find four hours later that the scorpions are dead, or almost lifeless, the alicorn is a good one, and there is not money enough in the world to pay for it. Otherwise, it is false."

Andrea Bacci tells how the Cardinal of Trent was generous in the use of the alicorn he owned by others, and once demonstrated with two pigeons its property of curing poison. Two pigeons were fed arsenic, but only one was given scrapings of the alicorn. They both became ill, but the pigeon given the scrapings recovered. The experiment was later repeated both with pigeons and kittens by John Wolenberg in 1636. He had the same success with the pigeons, but both kittens died.

The Reality, Mythology, and Fantasies of Unicorns

The illustration in Figure 28 came from Pierre Pomet's *History Générale des Drogues* published in 1694, in a chapter dedicated to the healing properties of the alicorn (*Cembalest, 9*).

The horn was good for more than just curing poison. According to Michael Valentini, the horn could also be used to cure rubella, measles, fevers, and pains. Andrea Bacci's *L'Alicorno*, published in 1573 and Laurent Catelan's *Histoire de la nature, chasse, vertus, proprietez et usage de la lycorne*, published in 1624, both expounded upon the fictional and fantastical uses to which the alicorn could be put.

Unfortunately for them and the world, the horn they were using was not a horn at all, but a tusk or tooth, and it had no medicinal or curative properties. If the horn of an actual unicorn did, we'll never know, as none have survived the long centuries.

Elizabeth I of England paid a small fortune for an alicorn. This was added to the Crown Jewels, and is known today as the Horn of Windsor. Her successor, James I, did the same. However, James I was suspicious he didn't possess the true article, so he poisoned a servant and gave him shavings from the horn as an antidote. When the servant died, he knew he'd been tricked. James I of England, who was also James IV of Scotland, wanted very much to have a genuine alicorn, as the unicorn was on his family's coat of arms: to symbolize the unity of the English monarchy with the Scottish monarchy, he had the unicorn symbol of Scotland placed on the royal coat of arms across from the English lion.

The confusion of the narwhal tusk and the alicorn ended rather abruptly in 1638, when Danish zoologist Ole Worm gave a public lecture on the true origin of most of the alicorns. While this led to a collapse in the narwhal tusk trade, it did nothing to the reputation of the "real" alicorn.

I was unable to find any references to the alicorn as a remedy for anything in Chinese sources. However, medieval Islamic authors, including Al-Biruni who wrote several books, credit the horn of the khutu as being an antidote to poison. He describes the horn as, "it is much in demand, and preserved in the treasuries among the Chinese who assert that it is a desirable article because the approach of poison causes it to exude" (*Ettinghausen, 114*). What is interesting is that earlier in his text, he compares the horn of a khutu bull to that of a tooth of a sea fish.

Ibn Al-Akfani indicates that the horn of a khutu, when combined with the vapors of perfume, has an excellent effect on hemorrhoids. He also writes that "the presence of poison in food is put to the test by it because when the broth or other dishes in the food are stirred with it the food cooks without fire, or if the horn is placed on a bowl it sweats without steam."

Al-Ghaffari, in his work on mineralogy in 1511, wrote that the horn of the hutu (a spelling variant) provides protection against poison for anyone who carries it with him. Poison placed near it will cause it to exude (*Ettinghausen, 114*).

Much like the European alicorn was in reality the tooth of the narwal, the khutu's horn is thought to be either a narwal tusk, or a walrus tusk, or even the tusk of a mammoth or elephant. These were used to make medieval Arabic knife handles, often traded to the Chinese, some of whom speculated regarding the animal from which the ivory came. One Chinese scholar imagined it came from a snake, as something poisonous would be the perfect cure for poison. Considering that the modern antidote to snake venom is made from snake venom, this is not such a far-fetched notion, other than that snakes don't grow horns of sufficient size.

However, it is good to know that the tooth of narwhal living in the waters off of Norway was widely traded across all of Europe, the Near East, and into China. Too commonly, the Middle Ages are thought of as a time of much isolation, and this demonstrates how global the trading was. The widespread traffic in this tusk, and the outrageous tale that this piece of bone could detect poison gave hope to the nervous across much of the medieval world.

Chris Lavers points out that Muslim knife makers made knife handles from khutu horns because, like the horn of the karkadan, they react to the presence of poison (*Lavers, 111*). Lavers argues that this is just another form of the same myth, a unicorn by yet another name. The curious thing is that he then looks to find out what exact material was used in the creation of these knives, sort of a hunt for the horn of the unicorn by the author.

In the end, the horn was also used for drinking. German poet Andreas Gryphius wrote, "We supped the bouquet of noble wine from gold and unicorn."

THE UNICORN IN ART AND LITERATURE

In reading through my prior chapters, you can see that the unicorn has been frequently represented in many different cultures' art. The unicorn was painted on cave walls in France, engraved into seals in both Mesopotamia and Harrapan India, carved in large reliefs in Persia, depicted in heraldry, sculpture, decorative household items, and embroidered in tapestries. I don't have the ability to do more than a brief survey of the artistic representation of the unicorn across culture and time, and so I've chosen what I believe to be significant works. Many of these inspired me in my own fiction. At the end of the chapter, I'll briefly review some other works of fiction which have featured a unicorn.

With deep regret, I was unable to find any visual representation of the unicorn in the pre-colonial art of the Americas. The single image I was able to find of the unicorn in sub-Saharan Africa is from Cosmas Indicopleustes, who visited Ethiopia in the mid fifth century CE (Figure 29). While I discussed his observations earlier in this book, the image itself is of interest, as it has clawed feet. This is somewhat unique in the depictions of unicorns.

THE REALITY, MYTHOLOGY, AND FANTASIES OF UNICORNS

The only representations I can find of the unicorn in the art of India is in many of the Indus Valley seals, which I've already covered in an earlier chapter. After the collapse of the Indus Valley civilization, the unicorn disappeared from the art of India. The unicorn seems to have been a favorite subject of European, Middle Eastern, and, to a lesser extent, Chinese and Japanese artists.

Figure 29. Unicorn illustration from Cosmas Indicopleustes.

While I've already shared with you a likely picture of elasmotherium by artists who may have seen it alive, there are four even older paintings of unicorns, found in Grotte de Lascaux, France.

The image in Figure 30 is one of the four, and it clearly shows the horn. There has been some criticism of those who call this a painting of a unicorn. Some claim that those who painted the figures on the walls of the caves painted just one horn because the animal is in profile; however, in the context of an image from the same cave painted in the same era, you can see that the artists knew perfectly well how to depict two horns on a profile if there should be a second horn (see, e.g., Figure 31).

There are over six hundred paintings in the cave, some representing fantastic composite creatures that combine different

Figure 30. Cave painting from Lascaux thought to be of a unicorn.

Figure 31. Cave painting from Lascaux showing aurochs and stags.

animals, or animals and humans. You also find depictions of large animals such as the auroch depicted in Figure 31.

From a chronological perspective, the next known depiction of a unicorn are the images found in Sumer and in the Indus Valley. I've shown some notable images from Sumerian, Indus Valley, and Assyrian seals in prior chapters.

The Reality, Mythology, and Fantasies of Unicorns

Figure 32. Unicorn bull from the Ishtar Gate, Babylon.

Interestingly enough, there is at least one ancient Mesopotamian seal that shows a divine hero fighting a winged unicorn (*Ettinghausen, 44*). This seal was dated to 1200 BCE, so the motif of the winged unicorn in Near Eastern art goes back to at least the middle Assyrian period of Mesopotamia, when it was quite common to find depictions of other winged creatures, such as winged bulls and winged horses.

There is a unicorn bull featured on the Ishtar gate of Babylon (Figure 32). The curve of the horn here is much like that of the horn of the unicorn seal of the Indus Valley. While some scholars think that this is a mosaic of a bull, others like to point out that the bull is often depicted in Babylonian art, and always with two horns even when in profile.

Other fantastic creatures found engraved on seals include that of a man-bull, similar to the myth of the minotaur in ancient Crete, and a human markhor composite with its spirally twisting horns. The Louvre has in its collection an Assyrian seal that contains a crowned person holding a dagger and the horn of a unicorn goat. The mouth of the unicorn touches a tree, and above the animal is the crescent moon. Brown believed that this seal depicted the king or god about to slay the creature in ritual combat (*Brown, 15*). Another such seal shows the

Assyrian god Bel with two unicorn goats. Above the unicorns is the crescent moon, and to the side of Bel is a palm tree. I've already discussed Brown's belief that the unicorn symbolizes the waning and waxing of the moon (*Brown, 17*).

A Phoenician gem found in Cnidos also shows the sun, the crescent moon, a star which Brown believes might be Venus, and the heads of a unicorn bull and cow (*Brown, 18*). The unicorn bull stands near a sacred tree. On the other side of the tree is a priest with a knife. Another Assyrian scene shows a man adoring a winged unicorn above which is the sun, the crescent moon, and seven stars. Brown reads this as cosmic harmony displayed visually.

In Achaemenid art, the depiction of the Divine figure, often the king, fighting the winged unicorn or other creature was one of many visual metaphors for the struggle between good and evil (*Von Der Osten, Henning, 232*). It is a shame that we don't know more about the art and its symbolism, as it is possible that this doesn't depict the king fighting evil, but rather his neighbors, the Assyrians, symbolized by the winged bull and winged unicorn found in Assyrian art.

The images of lions attacking unicorns found in Persia, which I've already shown in a prior chapter, are chronologically the next known images of unicorns. These images are again similar to what came before them, providing us a remarkably consistent view of the unicorn across cultures many centuries apart.

There are two known images of the unicorn in ancient Egyptian art. The first is a hieroglyph which appears to be either a unicorn or an antelope drawn in profile (*Bunsen, 514*). There are separate signs for a rhino, showing the horn on the nose, and the gazelle with two horns clearly depicted though the beast is drawn in profile.

The second comes from the Roman period, showing a lion and a unicorn playing the Roman game of lupus latrunculorum (Figure 34). The lion has won this contest (*Wright, 8*).

It is in medieval Islamic art that the imagination begins to run wild in the artistic portrayal of the unicorn. From the ninth through the seventeenth centuries CE, you find the unicorn depicted on a regular basis in Islamic literature, and in art from the tenth through the eighteenth century.

There is a delightful illustration of a unicorn fox in the Freer collection's copy of *Aja'ib Al-Makhluquat* by Al-Qazvini.

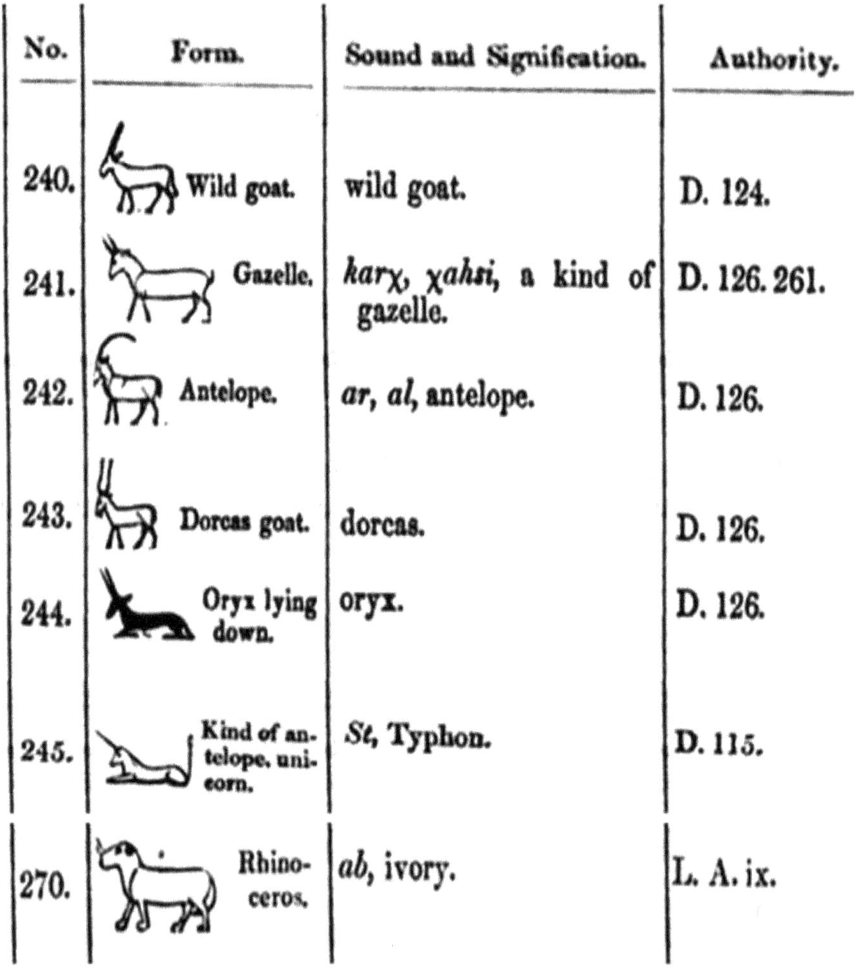

No.	Form.	Sound and Signification.	Authority.
240.	Wild goat.	wild goat.	D. 124.
241.	Gazelle.	karχ, χahsi, a kind of gazelle.	D. 126. 261.
242.	Antelope.	ar, al, antelope.	D. 126.
243.	Dorcas goat.	dorcas.	D. 126.
244.	Oryx lying down.	oryx.	D. 126.
245.	Kind of antelope, unicorn.	St, Typhon.	D. 115.
270.	Rhinoceros.	ab, ivory.	L. A. ix.

Figure 33. Hieroglyph to English dictionary.

The collection also has a lovely glass bowl that has a colorful design and features many real and fantastic creatures including wolves, hares, lions, stags, griffons, sphinxes, and unicorns racing around the bowl in eternal pursuit of each other (*Ettinghausen, 3*).

The image in Figure 35 shows an example of a winged unicorn. While the Museum of Fine Arts in Boston, where this illustration is housed, calls this *Alexander fights the rhinoceros of Habash*, the horn is clearly not on the nose, and no rhinoceros was ever born with wings. This unicorn has the feet of a lion, and the head of a dog. The neck is very much like that of a hyena. This illustration of a hero slaying a beast that could simply fly away, but doesn't,

Figure 34. Lion and unicorn playing lapus latrunculorum.

demonstrates that the medieval Islamic artist hadn't known the myth that unicorns were difficult to find and too swift to kill. The illustration above is from the *Shah-namah*, where the hero has to hunt and kill a unicorn. This particular image was painted in Tabriz, Iran, around 1335 CE. What is even more interesting is that many Islamic artists portray the unicorn as so fierce that it chases other animals, including elephants (*Ettinghausen, 30*).

Not all unicorns depicted in Islamic art had wings. On a plaque found on a door in the Madrasa Muquaddamīya in the city of Aleppo, you can see two antelope-like heads, each of which carries a single horn. The artist has shown each with two ears, so the choice to display a single horn is deliberate (*Ettinghausen, 5*). However, the absence of wings may be due to the incomplete representation of the body.

Another unicorn without wings is found in the Persian *Manāfi* manuscript painted in Marāgha at the end of the thirteenth century. This unicorn is rather bovine in appearance, much like the unicorns found in more ancient art in the region (*Ettinghausen, 9*).

There are other manuscripts that depict the unicorn multiple times in the same document, sometimes with wings, sometimes without. A *Mu'nis Al-Ahrār* miniature of 1341 shows the elephant, roc (a huge carnivorous bird common to Islamic stories), and a winged karkadan together. This echoes the famous story as relayed by Al-Bīrūni that the karkadan will attack the elephant, impaling it with its horn, but that both are

THE REALITY, MYTHOLOGY, AND FANTASIES OF UNICORNS

Figure 35. Firdawsi's *Shahnama*: Alexander fights the rhinoceros of Habash.

prey to the roc (*Ettinghausen, 31*). This story is also found in certain versions of the Arabian Nights.

The illustration in Figure 36, now housed in the Metropolitan Museum of Art's collection, is from the thirteenth century manuscript *Aja'ib Al-Makhluqat wa Ghara'ib Al-Mawjudat*. It shows a pink-spotted karkadan. The horn has sprouting branches and looks somewhat like a flame. The text, written by Al-Qazwini, explains that since the horn was an effective antidote to poison, it was used to make knife handles.

In China, much of the art we have of the unicorn (qilin) is sculptural rather than drawn, painted, or engraved. As the qilin was sent from the gods, it is no surprise that an incense burner would be shaped in the likeness of a qilin. The sculpture shown in Figure 37 is from the Ming dynasty, though we don't know when in the almost three hundred years of the Ming dynasty it was made.

Often the qilin were depicted as dragon-like, scaled, but with the torso of a horse or bull, and with a single horn. Sometimes the horn was depicted with branches (Figure 38).

Figure 36. Image from the *Aja'ib Al-Makhluqat wa Ghara'ib Al-Mawjudat.*

In Japan, the unicorn is known as the kiren or kirin as an alternative transliteration into English, which is itself a transliteration of qilin. These are frequently depicted in both sculptural and pictoral art. One famous painting of the kiren graces Kirin beer. You can find kiren netsuke (small carved ornaments worn as a part of traditional Japanese dress) which look much like the winged karkadan of Islam or the winged unicorns of ancient Assyria. The kiren often appears tiger-like in artwork, but has the body of a deer, the tail of an ox; the body is covered with the scales of a fish and, of course, it has a single horn.

Turning my attention now to the unicorn in European art, I find a rich field with many images. Martin Schongauer's *Mystic Hunt of the Unicorn,* 1489, shows a diminutive brown unicorn in Mary's lap in a loving depiction of the Annunciation. The horn, also brown, is almost as long as the unicorn itself (*Leibowitz*). You can see God in the heavens, Jesus carrying the

Figure 37. Qilin incense burner.

cross flying down to her, and the Holy Spirit in the form of the dove. The hunting dogs would have driven the unicorn to her.

Schongauer was a noted fifteenth-century engraver and painter from the Alsatian region of the Alps. His work was well respected by his contemporaries, and one of his engravings was copied by Michelangelo. He was strongly influenced by contemporary German and Dutch art. While young, he had been sent to the University of Leipzig, perhaps to study for the priesthood or to study law. His only dated painting, *Madonna in the Rose Garden*, and other undated paintings were inspired by Christian mythology and beliefs.

Figure 38. Qing Qilin.

Figure 39. Kiren Netsuke.

The image in Figure 41, a fifteenth century allegorical painting by Francesco Di Giorgio Martini, entitled *Castità e unicorno*, shows the unicorn as an ugly and fierce creature submitting to chastity's caress. This painting inspired me to substitute chastity for virginity in my novel, *The Garden at the Roof of the World*, as the virtue that unicorns looked for in humans. Francesco Di

Figure 40. Mystic Hunt of the Unicorn.

The Reality, Mythology, and Fantasies of Unicorns

Giorgio Martini is far from unique in painting Chastity in the company of a unicorn. Chastity is a more complex virtue than virginity, as it encourages sex once a couple is wed.

This next painting by Francesco Giorgio Martini in 1463 (Figure 42) shows two unicorns pulling Chastity on a chariot behind Cupid, whose wings are clipped. Chastity here is shown triumphant over Cupid, who is a metaphor for sexual desire.

Martini lived in Siena, studying painting from Vecchietta. Much of his career was focused on architecture, including even writing on the subject. He was active at a time of much warfare between the cities of Italy and helped design and construct a series of fortifications.

In 1491, someone made this delightful woodcut of a unicorn and a ram and published it in the *Meshal ha-Kadmoni* (Figure 43).

The *Meshal ha-Kadmoni*, or fable of the ancients, is a collection of Jewish fables, written by the poet, cabbalist, and physician Isaac ben Solomon ibn Sahula in the thirteenth century. He aimed

Figure 41. Castità e unicorno.

Figure 42. Triumph of Chastity.

to create Jewish stories in the style of *Kalilah and Dimnah*, a collection of fables originating in India, and the *Voyages of Sinbad the Sailor*, which were very popular with medieval Jewish readers. His stories have both animal and human protagonists and were illustrated. Each starts with the words of a cynic against one of the main virtues: wisdom, penitence, sound counsel, and humility. The surviving manuscripts all come from southern Germany. This image is from a story discussing the wickedness of hunters.

Figure 43. Unicorn and Ram.

The Reality, Mythology, and Fantasies of Unicorns

It isn't just well-dressed ladies of station and notable women of religion and mythology that you find depicted with unicorns in European art. One of my favorites, from a sixteenth century tapestry currently found in the Historisches Museum Basel, is called *Wild Woman with a Unicorn* (Figure 44). This image was one of the tapestries that inspired me in the writing of *The Garden at the Roof of the World*.

There is a modern group of musicians, Heliotrope, who featured a copy of this art on the cover of their album, *The Romance of the Rose*. This album features music from women troubadours and trouvères of the eleventh and twelfth centuries CE. I would often listen to their music while writing the novel. One major character, Elise, would have known this music and sung many of the songs in her life. The image itself inspired a scene in my story where Gwenaella, the heroine of the story, goes a little wild and is in desperate need of help.

No less famous than the Unicorn Tapestries found today in the collection of the Cloisters in New York, New York, are the

Figure 44. Wild Woman with a Unicorn.

six fifteenth century Flemish tapestries called *The Lady and the Unicorn*. Here we find our rivals, the lion and the unicorn, co-existing peacefully with a lady. My personal favorite of the six shows the woman, sitting, with the unicorn snuggling up to her. She is showing the unicorn its reflection in a mirror.

An enchanting modern recording of music from the *Montpellier Codex* by the musical group Anonymous 4 has this image as its cover art. I frequently listened to this as I wrote my novel, since this would have been music familiar to Élise.

The tapestries themselves are likely allegorical in nature and may represent the five senses (*Beer, 153*). The arms in the banner, the three crescents, belonged to the Le Viste family. The unicorn could have been added as a play on words, perhaps intended to stand for vitesse, which means speed. They may well have been intended to celebrate the wedding of Claudia Le Viste with a Jean de Chabannes, whose nickname was "Lion's cub" (*Beer, 154*). There are other theories. Regardless, the tapestries are well beloved, and have had such authors as George

Figure 45. The Lady and the Unicorn: Sight.

Sands, Marcel Proust, and Rainer Maria Rilke feature the tapestries in their own art.

The fifteenth century treasured the idea of the unicorn as a purifier of water. To this end, someone had a water dispenser made in the shape of a unicorn (Figure 46). It is unknown if this was used for washing one's hands at Mass or before a meal, but I have to wonder if there isn't a fragment of a unicorn "horn" inside of this to "purify" the water dispensed (*Sooke, 2018*).

Even in European art, the unicorn is not always portrayed as virtuous or as a metaphor for Jesus. In 1516, Albrecht Dürer created a masterful engraving that shows the abduction of a woman by a man riding a unicorn. Many art historians (*Leibowitz*) believe that this engraving is an illustration of the ancient Greek myth of Hades's abduction of Persephone. What is interesting is that many mythologists believe that the Persephone myth is inspired by the Erishkigal myth from Sumer, and we've already seen that unicorns may be linked to the Erishkigal cult, and were associated with the underworld in certain Christian sects.

Dürer worked in Nuremberg in the later half of the fifteenth and early sixteenth centuries. He maintained a close relationship with major Italian artists of the era, including Raphael, Bellini, and da Vinci. He was patronized by Emperor Maximilian I of the Holy Roman Empire, and is commemorated

Figure 46. Fifteenth century water container.

by the Lutheran church, which was established while he was active as an artist. He wrote extensively on the principles of mathematics, perspective, and ideal proportions.

Jean Duvet depicted the dangers of having unicorns around without the virgin to tame them in this powerful engraving showing a unicorn in pursuit of a king. Here you see the unicorn killing the king's guards while in hot pursuit of the hapless king.

Duvet is mostly known for his engravings and was the first significant French printmaker. His style is influenced by a journey to Italy in the early sixteenth century. He was well respected by both Francis I and Henry II, kings of France, who appointed him their goldsmith. He supported the Catholic cause in a time when nations were fighting the Wars of Religion. While the above piece is not flattering of monarchy, one of his better known works are three plates he made for Henry II celebrating the mystique of divine monarchy.

Figure 47. The abduction on a Unicorn.

The Reality, Mythology, and Fantasies of Unicorns

Figure 48. Untitled engraving of a unicorn attacking the King and his guard.

The print of the unicorn shown in Figure 48 is one of six prints he made on the subject and he was known as the "Unicorn Master" from the quality of his prints. His work is largely inspired by art of the Middle Ages, though like other artists of the era, he worked to depict the human form with accuracy and in proper proportions.

Raphael famously painted a lovely woman holding a diminutive unicorn in *Young Woman with Unicorn*, likely created in 1506 (Figure 49). In the original painting, found in an x-ray of the finished painting, the woman held a lap dog where the unicorn now sits. This may account somewhat for the size of the unicorn. The presence of the unicorn may have been to indicate that the woman was a virgin. The painting may have been commissioned for a wedding, or in the hopes of a proposal of marriage. The lap dog was a common symbol for fidelity (*Leibowitz*). The painting today can be found in the Borghese Gallery.

Figure 50 shows the Borromeo family icon, the unicorn, in battle with a lion. This is a close-up detail from one of the seven tapestries collectively called *The Unicorn Collection*, created in about 1565. You can find these hanging in the Salone deli Arazzi in the Palazzo Borromeo. Not only does it depict the unicorn triumphant over the lion, but the unicorn has cloven hooves, a beard like that of a goat, and the head and body of a horse.

Figure 49. Virgin and Unicorn.

The family also had a statue of a unicorn being ridden by Cupid on the roof of their palace (*Walsh*).

The family were originally merchants who became landowners and aristocrats, eventually organizing an independent state within the Duchy of Milan. They were active Catholics, and a number of cardinals were Borromeo. Their family crest features a unicorn in a red field with golden flames, and from them the unicorn became featured on crests of many relations through marriage.

An even later depiction of the unicorn that combines goat and horse-like features is the painting by Annibale Carracci, painted in about 1602 (Figure 51). The woman is Giulia Farnese, mistress to Pope Alexander VI. The unicorn looks completely distressed, but the woman appears to delight in comforting the poor beast (*WikiArt*). It is not the only image of Guilia Farnese with a unicorn; there is another such painting by the artist Luca Longhi. As she was married to Orsino Orsini before her affair with Pope Alexander VI, she was apparently neither virginal nor chaste when either painting was made, and was commonly called the Pope's whore. It is quite likely that these paintings were commissioned to attempt to defend her reputation and refute the rumored affair.

A more modern look at the interesting relationship between the unicorn and virginity is Gustave Moreau's *Les Licornes*, painted in 1887 (Figure 52). Here we have three unicorns of various sizes cozying up to some women, one of whom is essentially naked, but depicted in a regal pose. Moreau is regarded as a symbolist and was heavily influenced by both the Italian Renaissance and by exotic subjects. This painting was inspired by the tapestries known as *The Lady and the Unicorn*. The lily held by the lady is a symbol of purity, the clothing contains images of other fabulous animals and of combats, and the chalice may have been intended to be the Holy Grail.

Betye Saar used the common understanding of the unicorn as an animal that validates the worth of the woman to make a powerful statement about black women in her 1960 painting, *To Catch a Unicorn* (Figure 53). The painting shows a confident nude woman leaning back against a unicorn slightly smaller than herself.

Figure 50. Tapestry, Palazzo Borromeo.

Figure 51. Virgin and Unicorn.

They are both illuminated by the twin lights of both moon and sun (*Leibowitz*). The painter was fascinated by the mystical and wove an exploration of mystical elements in much of her work in the 1960s, the same moon and sun that have been part of the images depicting the unicorn for six thousand years.

Damien Hirst, in his 2008 sculpture *The Dream*, shows the unicorn one expects from Hollywood movies, a large white horse with a long horn. The "fictitious" beast is encased in formaldehyde and glass, like some of his other taxidermy artwork. The unicorn is a real foal, with an artificial horn placed on its head (Leibowitz).

Rebecca Horn, perhaps using her name as a pun, created a video of herself dressed as a unicorn entitled *Unicorn* in 1970–1972. Wearing a horn on her head and a full body harness that held the horn in place, but nothing else, she is at once the unicorn and the naked woman who entices the unicorn out of hiding to come and rest with her (*Leibowitz*). The model spent the day walking back and forth along a path through the woods and through a field.

The Reality, Mythology, and Fantasies of Unicorns

Figure 52. Les Licornes.

There is a ballet dedicated to the unicorn created by Jean Cocteau in 1953. This ballet tells a story inspired by "The Lady and the Unicorn" tapestries.

Turning to literature, the unicorn is most famously found in Peter Beagle's *The Last Unicorn*. A unicorn briefly helps the character Alianora in Poul Anderson's *Three Hearts and Three Lions*. After losing a battle with a lion for the throne, a unicorn helps Tristian and Yvaine in Neil Gaiman's *Stardust*. The only named unicorn in Narnia is Jewel in C.S. Lewis' *The Last Battle*, though Peter rides one into battle in the movie version of *The Lion, the Witch and the Wardrobe*. Roger Zelazny has a unicorn playing chess in his *Unicorn Variation*, published in *Asimov's* in 1981. There are innumerable unicorns in picture books for children, and they feature in movies such as *Legend*, *Harry Potter and the Sorcerer's Stone*, *Tropico*, and many others. The unicorn has become a common symbol of innocence and its loss in contemporary fiction.

There is one chivalric romance that is about a unicorn. The ballad, *de la Dame a la Lycorne et du Biau Chevalier au Lyon*,

Figure 53. To Catch a Unicorn.

(*Beer, 151*) tells the story of a good and noble woman who is given a unicorn. Some believe that this ballad is inspired by the *Lady and the Unicorn* tapestries, but there is nothing in the tapestries to link them back to this story.

There is also a delightful folk story about a unicorn saving an old and wise woman near the aptly named Einhornhöle in the Harz mountains. The cave contained at one point the bones of as many as seventy species of animals, some of which were once believed to be unicorn bones.

In most of these stories, the unicorn is only a supporting character, often unnamed, just a beast helping others. This is part of what made *The Last Unicorn* by Peter Beagle so special: at long last, the unicorn had a story that was about a unicorn on a quest of her own, to restore other unicorns in the world.

The reality, mythology, and fantasies of Unicorns

In my own novel, *The Garden at the Roof of the World*, I also give a unicorn a quest of her own, to save the life of her father, the unicorn who walked with Adam and Eve in Eden.

MAKING UNICORNS

In 1796, Le Vailant described a process, long known to animal herders, of manipulating the horns of a young animal so that they grow together, with the points meeting over the center of the forehead. The end result is an animal that has a horn that looks like the unicorn's. W. Franklin Dove, a biologist at the University of Maine, was able to explain how this works. Horns don't grow from the skull, but from tissues located above the bones. The horn buds will eventually fuse to the skeleton underneath but can be manipulated while the animal is too young for the horn to have fused.

W. Franklin Dove was able to verify that this technique was behind the flock of "unicorn sheep" that was presented to King George V of England while he was still Prince of Wales in 1906. In 1911, the Nepalese prime minister, Maharajah Chandra Jang explained to the British how the horns are trained to grow together through cutting and manipulation. The cruel process consists of taking a hot iron to the horns when the lambs are two to three months of age. You then treat the wounds with a mixture of oil and soot. This is traditionally practiced on the barwal, a breed of heavy horned sheep commonly found in Tibet.

THE REALITY, MYTHOLOGY, AND FANTASIES OF UNICORNS

Figure 54. Barwal sheep with single horn.

W. Franklin Dove experimented on a bull calf of not more than a day old. He cut the calf's horn buds, while leaving them attached to skin to ensure that they'd stay alive. He then planted the buds one on top of the other in a prepared area in the center of the forehead. This was a success. After two years of growth, the horn curved slightly upward toward the tip, gracefully extending the curve of the back and neck when the animal stood at attention. The horn completely grafted itself in the bone of the forehead. It was white at the base and black at the tip. Had Dove used a cow instead of a bull, the horn would have had a red tip, as the color is linked to gender in the breed he used in his experiment.

If you remember from the first chapter of this volume, Ctesias of Cnidus had described the horn of the unicorn as white at the base, black in the middle, and red at the tip. It is possible that Ctesias had seen an animal that had been modified in just such a manner. If the practice was carried out in Persia with the auroch, they would have possibly produced the unicorns depicted so frequently in their art. Pliny, in book 11 of his *Natural History*, describes a slightly different process of horn modification, without linking it to making a unicorn, out of cattle, sheep, or goats.

Dove hypothesized that animals modified in such a way would naturally become the leaders of the herd, as their horn could do real damage in a fight between two animals. In herds of cattle where there are both horned and unhorned cattle, the unhorned cattle have dominance over the horned cattle, so I'm not certain that

Dove's hypothesis would bear out in reality. Today, both the Nuer and the Dinka modify the horns of their cattle and mark the leader of the herd through such modification. However, neither the Dinka's nor the Nuer's horn modifications produce a unicorn, and the leadership of the herd is more ceremonial than practical. They often will decorate such a horn with a bell strung between the two horns using horse hair. There is evidence that the modification of cattle horns was even practiced in ancient Egypt (*Essam, Hoda, 168*).

Lydekker in his 1912 monograph on *The Breeds of Asiatic Highlands* had in fact observed that two-horned barwal rams are used on a regular basis for fighting, but one-horned rams are created to be sold to wealthy patrons in Nepal (*Lydekker, 163*). Rather than enhancing the fighting prowess of the animal, changing the horn structure so that the ram only has one horn makes it less capable as a fighter.

Many fortunes have been made over the centuries from fraudulently representing things as associated with or being unicorns. As discussed before, narwal tusks used to be sold at a fortune, with myths to enhance the value of the sold product. Unicorn sheep are still produced for sale to wealthy patrons where the two-horned variety is the same beast available at much lower prices. The unicorn industry has been ripe with fraud for who knows how many centuries.

It is sad, in a way, to end this particular quest for the unicorn on such a jaded note, but the unicorn in the modern era has become little more than a symbol of rare and uniquely successful companies and a toy for young children, too innocent to be jaded by the lack of any deeper significance regarding the unicorns they love so much.

Yet, the unicorn is the symbol of the Boston Athletic Association, the organization that organizes the Boston Marathon annually. The success of movies such as *Legend* and *The Last Unicorn* shows that stories about the loss of unicorns move us deeply. There are reasons the wealthy will spend more to have even a fraudulent unicorn; on one level, we all long for what the unicorn has been for human society. For better or worse, the unicorn has been inspiring human artists and storytellers for about 20,000 years, and the recent discoveries of both elasmotherium and the drawing of it on cave walls in France speak to the power of that inspiration.

The last photograph I'll leave you with is that of a recent installation of an Elasmotherium reconstruction at the

The reality, mythology, and fantasies of Unicorns

Figure 55. Elasmotherium reconstruction at the Ústí Museum.

Ústí Museum (Figure 55). This will give you a sense of the scale of both the beast and its horn. If none of the creatures survived into the historical era, the impact of its memory on the human psyche is both unmeasurable and unmatched.

I remain a naive optimist that some of these creatures survived long enough to confuse Marco Polo, expecting to find the unicorn of mythology and encountering the unicorn of reality. Unless something turns up in the archaeological record, all we have are ancient texts that point vaguely in this direction.

In the transforming of my notes into this volume, I've encountered unicorns everywhere I turn. From balloon unicorns in the local market, toy unicorns in the Frankfurt airport, unicorns in art museums and even at information security conferences where the Electronic Frontier Foundation proudly sold unicorn-decorated t-shirts to raise funds. I am blessed that this perplexing creature has figured in both my fiction and in my life.

As I learned of how the unicorn was understood in so many times and places, my affection for the creature grew. I am not pure of heart, so I have no hope of encountering a unicorn outside of history, art, fiction and mythology. I can but hope that perhaps, in what wild spaces still exist in our world and in our hearts, a unicorn can be found.

IMAGES

Figure 1: Sketch of Elasmotherium by Rashevsky, 1878. https://en.wikipedia.org/wiki/Elasmotherium

Figure 2: Drawing believed to be Elasmotherium, Rouffignac cave, France. https://en.wikipedia.org/wiki/Elasmotherium

Figure 3: Map of known range of Elasmotherium's habitat, from Schvyreva, A.K. *On the importance of the representatives of the genus Elasmotherium (Rhinocerotidae, Mammalia) in the biochronology of the Pleistocene of Eastern Europe.* Elsevier. May 16, 2015.

Figure 4: Roe deer with one antler. (© Center of Natural Sciences, Prata, Italy)

Figure 5: Unicorn and Lion from Ukrainian Synagogue. https://kinneretstern.files.wordpress.com/2015/03/tumblr_nkkgji-wmgs1s67vtvo1_1280.jpg

Figure 6: Unicorn Rabbit (al Miraj) https://upload.wikimedia.org/wikipedia/commons/7/78/Al-miraj_and_Serpent.png

Figure 7: Qilin https://www.marcmaison.com/architecturAl-antiques-resources/unicorn

Figure 8: Indus Valley Seal

https://www.harappa.com/category/slide-subject/seals

Figure 9: Unicorn figurine found at Chanhu-daro https://www.harappa.com/sites/default/files/pdf/Kenoyer2013%20Indus%20Unicorns-1.pdf

Figure 10: Procession of unicorns and lions from Persepolis. https://www.gettyimages.com/detail/photo/procession-of-unicorns-and-lions-at-high-res-stock-photography/518987488

Figure 11: One of a number of figures from a victory parade panel from the Ishtar temple at Mari, Parpola, page 439

Figure 12: Statite stamp with human headed composite creature with bovine horns from Mohenjo-daro. Aruz, (30)

Figure 13: Queen of the Night, Albenda (172)

Figure 14: Merodach, or Bel, armed for the conflict with the dragon, Smith and Sayce https://www.gutenberg.org/files/60559/60559-h/60559-h.htm#Chapter_VI (112)

Figure 15: Cylinder seal found in the Shara Temple, Tell Agrab http://www.layish.co.uk/catalogue_e_1_art_history.pdf (9)

Figure 16: Rock relief found in Malatia (in Modern Armenia) showing the Assyrian gods in procession https://digitalcollections.nypl.org/items/510d47e2-f667-a3d9-e040-e00a18064a99/book?parent=f1a4e960-c6d3-012f-b5b0-58d385a7bc34#page/53/mode/2up

Figure 17: Close-up on part of the Black Obelisk of Shalmaneser III. http://bharatkalyan97.blogspot.com/2019/06/nimrud-kalhu-black-obelisk-with-indus.html

Figure 18: Terracotta relief of Ishtar with wings from Larsa (second millennium BC) https://commons.wikimedia.org/wiki/File:Winged_goddess-AO6501-IMG_0638-black.jpg

Figure 19: Cylinder seal impression from the Elamite capital of Susa, http://articles.adsabs.harvard.edu/cgi-bin/nph-iarticle_query?bibcode=1998JBAA..108....9R&db_key=AST&page_ind=1&plate_select=NO&data_type=GIF&type=SCREEN_GIF&classic=YES, Rogers, 108

Figure 20: Sumerian seal showing Inanna, Utu, and Enki. Kramer, *Sumerian Mythology* plate VII

Figure 21: This partial gameboard from Ur is made of engraved shell plaques, limestone, and lapis lazuli. PM object B16742.

The reality, mythology, and fantasies of Unicorns

Figure 22: Albrech Dürer's *Ritter, Tod und Teufel* https://commons.wikimedia.org/wiki/File:Duerer_-_Ritter,_Tod_und_Teufel_(Der_Reuther).jpg

Figure 23: Statue of girl with unicorn from Vigeland Park in Oslo https://www.pxfuel.com/en/free-photo-jzxzg

Figure 24: *The Unicorn Reborn* https://commons.wikimedia.org/wiki/File:The_Unicorn_in_Captivity_(from_the_Unicorn_Tapestries)_%E2%80%93_467642.jpg

Figure 25: *The Annunciation as an Allegorical Unicorn Hunt*, ca.1500, 5 1/8 x 7 ½ in., The Morgan Library &Museum, MS M.1201, Photography by Janny Chiu, 2017 https://guenther-rarebooks.com/artworks/categories/2/9429/

Figure 26: Bosch, Hieronymus. *The Garden of Earthly Delights* https://commons.wikimedia.org/w/index.php?curid=147998

Figure 27: http://tabisite.com/photo/97ir/srze.shtml

Figure 28: Pierre Pomet's *History Générale des drogues* published in 1694 https://www.metmuseum.org/art/collection/search/479709

Figure 29: Cosmas Indicopleustes, http://www.tertullian.org/fathers/cosmas15-plate09.gif

Figure 30: Cave painting of unicorn https://en.wikipedia.org/wiki/Lascaux#/media/File:Lascaux_II.jpg

Figure 31: Cave painting of aurocs and stags https://en.wikipedia.org/wiki/Lascaux#/media/File:Lascaux_painting.jpg

Figure 32: https://commons.wikimedia.org/wiki/File:One_of_the_aurochs_of_the_the_Ishtar_Gate_of_Babylon,_colored_glazed_and_molded_bricks,_6th_century_BCE._Pergamon_Museum.jpg

Figure 33: hieroglyphs from *Egypt's Place in Universal History* https://www.google.com/books/edition/_/JpBJAAAAMAAJ?hl=en&gbpv=0

Figure 34: Lion and unicorn playing a game of lupus latrunculorum https://www.google.com/books/edition/A_History_of_Caricature_and_Grotesque_in/Pos741KQFtcC?hl=en&gbpv=1&printsec=frontcover

Figure 35: Firdawsi's *Shahnama: Alexander fights the rhinoceros of Habash* https://collections.mfa.org/objects/17580

Figure 36: Aja'ib Al-Makhluqat wa Ghara'ib Al-Mawjudat https://www.metmuseum.org/art/collection/search/479711

Figure 37: Qilin incense burner https://www.amnh.org/var/ezflow_site/storage/images/media/amnh/images/exhibitions/past-exhibitions/mythic-creatures/4qilin-incense-burner_med.jpg/235652-1-eng-US/4qilin-incense-burner_med.jpg.jpg

Figure 38: Qing Qilin https://en.wikipedia.org/wiki/Qilin#/media/File:QingQilin.jpg

Figure 39: Netsuke in the shape of a kirin https://japanesemythology.files.wordpress.com/2014/11/netsuke-powerful-kirin-figurine.jpg

Figure 40: Martin Schongauer's *Mystic Hunt of the Unicorn*, 1489. https://commons.wikimedia.org/wiki/File:Unicorn_hunt_-_Martin_Schongauer_(circle).jpg

Figure 41: *Castità e unicorno*. https://commons.wikimedia.org/wiki/File:Francesco_di_Giorgio,_castit%C3%A0_e_unicorno.jpg

Figure 42: Triumph of Chastity https://commons.wikimedia.org/wiki/File:Triumph-chastity-francesco-d-giorgio-martini-1463-8.JPG

Figure 43: Unicorn and Ram https://www.metmuseum.org/art/collection/search/479689

Figure 44: "Wild Woman" with unicorn https://www.hmb.ch/en/museums/objects-in-the-collection/details/s/wild-woman-with-unicorn/

Figure 45: *The Lady and the Unicorn: Sight*. https://en.wikipedia.org/wiki/The_Lady_and_the_Unicorn#/media/File:The_Lady_and_the_unicorn_Sight.jpg

Figure 46: Fifteenth century water container. https://ychef.files.bbci.co.uk/1600x900/p06vldg1.jpg

Figure 47: *The Abduction on a Unicorn*. https://www.clevelandart.org/art/1963.469

Figure 48: Untitled engraving of a unicorn attacking the King and his guard https://www.harvardartmuseums.org/collections/object/299868?position=0

Figure 49: *Young Woman with Unicorn*. https://en.wikipedia.org/wiki/Young_Woman_with_Unicorn

Figure 50: Detail from one of the seven Borromeo tapestries. https://innerspaceinteriordesign.com/wp-content/uploads/2011/09/Converted_file_8e68bc0d.png.jpg

The reality, mythology, and fantasies of Unicorns

Figure 51: *Virgin and Unicorn.* https://www.wikiart.org/en/annibale-carracci/virgin-and-unicorn-a-virgin-with-a-unicorn-1605

Figure 52: *Les Licornes*
https://en.musee-moreau.fr/object/unicorns-les-licornes

Figure 53: *To Catch a Unicorn*
https://www.moma.org/collection/works/284137

Figure 54: Barwal sheep with single horn
https://i.kinja-img.com/gawker-media/image/upload/c_fit,f_auto,fl_progressive,pg_1,q_80,w_470/988635472545993509.jpg

Figure 55: Elasmotherium reconstruction. https://1v1d1e1lmiki1lgcvx32p49h8fe-wpengine.netdna-ssl.com/wp-content/uploads/2018/11/1543257499-siberian-unicorn.jpg

BIBLIOGRAPHY

While many of the works I used in my research are available in print, they are even more readily available on the internet. Where I used a print source that is also available via URL, I will list the URL, as some of these sources are hard to find in libraries.

Albenda, Pauline. "The 'Queen of the Night' Plaque: A Revisit". *Journal of the American Oriental Society*, Vol. 125, No. 2 (Apr. –Jun., 2005), pp. 171–190
https://www.jstor.org/stable/20064325

Aelian. Scholfield, A. F. Translator. *On the Nature of Animals*. http://www.attalus.org/translate/animals4.html#52 1958

Aristotle, *The History of Animals*. Translated by D'Arcy Wentworth Thompson.
http://classics.mit.edu/Aristotle/history_anim.2.ii.html

Aruz, Joan. Editor. *Art of the First Cities*. The Metropolitan Museum of Art. New York, 2003

Aruz, Joan, "Reflections on Fantastic Beasts of the Hrappan World." *Walking with the Unicorn*, Archaeopress, Oxford. 2018 pages 26-32.

Bacci, Andrea. *L'Alicorno*. https://www.classicistranieri.com/andrea-bacci-lalicorno-pdf.html
I used the translation, found here: http://www.attalus.org/translate/animals4.html by A.F.Scholfield (1958) Paragraph 53

Beer, Rüdiger Robert. *Unicorn Myth and Reality*. James J. Kerry Inc. New York, 1977

Beneditti, Giocomo "Which Animal was the Unicorn of the Indus Seals?" *New Indology*. 2014. http://new-indology.blogspot.com/2014/03/which-animAl-was-unicorn-of-indus-seals.html

Benedetti, Giacomo. "The Story of Ekaśṛṅga in the Mahāvastu with its parallels". *Journal of Asian Civilizations*. Vol. 38 No. 1. July 2015 http://www.academia.edu/30448353/The_story_of_Eka%C5%9B%E1%B9%9B%E1%B9%85ga_in_the_Mah%C4%81vastu_with_its_parallels

Berlin, Adele and Brettler, Marc Zvi. Editors. *The Jewish Study Bible*. Jewish Publication Society. Tanakh Translation. Oxford University Press, Oxford, 2004.

Betz, Hans Dieter. "Fragments from a Catabasis Ritual in a Greek Magical Papyrus", *History of Religions* 19,4 (May 1980):287-295

Black, Jeremy and Green, Anthony. *Gods, Demons, and Symbols of Ancient Mesopotamia*. University of Texas Press, Austin. 1992

Brown, Robert. *The Unicorn, A Mythological Investigation*. https://www.sacred-texts.com/etc/tu/index.htm

Bunt, C. (1930). *The Lion and the Unicorn*. Antiquity, 4(16), 425-437

Caesar, C.J. *De Bello Gallico*. Project Gutenberg; Everyman's Library version, 1915 edition, translated by W.A. MacDevitt. http://www.gutenberg.org/cache/epub/10657/pg10657-images.html

Caspers, E. C. L. During. "The Indus Valley 'Unicorn': A Near Eastern Connection?" *Journal of the Economic and Social History of the Orient*, vol. 34, no. 4, 1991, pp. 312–350. JSTOR, www.jstor.org/stable/3632455.

Cowie, Ashley. "Legends of the Unicorn Horn: cures, antidotes, and medicinal magic". *Ancient Origins*. 2018. https://www.ancient-origins.net/myths-legends/magic-unicorn-horn-0010750

Curley, Michael, translator. *Physiologus: A Medieval Book of Nature Lore*. University of Chicago Press, 2009. https://books.google.com/books?id=I3tUyc7vVlAC&pg=PA51&lpg=PA51&dq=Physiologus+unicorn

+online&source=bl&ots=pkxrxcH0Ck&sig=ACfU3U0geSfde2ESJ92h-6nVEmo3hPF7dQ&hl=en&ppis=_e&sa=X&ved=2ahUKEwi8_9bR1I7oAhXghXIEHX5dAQcQ6AEwBXoECAoQAQ#v=onepage&q=Physiologus%20unicorn%20online&f=false

Duerst, J. Ulrich (1899), *Die rinder von babylonien, Assyrien und Ägypten und ihr zusammenhang mit den rindern der alten welt.* Berlin, p. 9

Edwards, C.J.; Magee, D.A.; Park, S.D.E.; McGettigan, P.A.; Lohan, A.J.; et al. (2010). "A Complete Mitochondrial Genome Sequence from a Mesolithic Wild Aurochs (Bos primigenius)"". *PLoS ONE.* 5 (2): e9255. Bibcode:2010PLoSO...5.9255E. doi:10.1371/journal.pone.0009255. PMC 2822870. PMID 20174668

Elsafeed, Essam; Khalifa, Hoda. "A Comparative Study of Modified Animal Horns in Ancient Egypt and Modern African Tribes." *Geography*, 2017. https://pdfs.semanticscholar.org/aaa4/21ade601c150cfffd51a258c967c45d660f6.pdf

Elmer G. Suhr Source: *Folklore*, Vol. 75, No. 2 (Summer, 1964), pp. 91-109 Published by Taylor & Francis, Ltd. on behalf of Folklore Enterprises, Ltd. Stable URL: https://www.jstor.org/stable/1258042 Accessed: 19-05-2020 01:52 UTC

Elsby, Liz, "The Wooden Synagogue of Chodorow" Yad Vashem. https://www.yadvashem.org/articles/general/wooden-synagogue-of-chodorow.html

Encyclopedia of Prehistory, Springer, 2003 pages 179-190

Ettinghausen, Richard. *The Unicorn: Studies in Muslim Iconography.* Freer Gallery of Art. 1950 https://archive.org/details/unicorn00etti/mode/2up

Faculty of Oriental Studies. *Gilgameš, Enkidu and the nether world*, University of Oxford, The Electronic Text Corpus of Sumerian Literature. 2003

Fischer, Louis-Paul; Fischer Véronique Cossu Ferra. "La licorne et la corne de licorne chez les apothicaires et les Médecins". *Historie Des Sciences Medicales*, Tome XLV No. 3. 2011. https://www.biusante.parisdescartes.fr/sfhm/hsm/HSMx2011x045x003/HSMx2011x045x003x0265.pdf

Freeman, Margaret. *The Unicorn Tapestries.* Metropolitan Museum of Art. 1976.

https://books.google.com/books?id=ATbO6lv4LsMC&pg=PA57&lpg=PA57&dq=Chastity+and+the+unicorn&source=bl&ots=uBXofrGR-m&sig=ACfU3U0GACWxHcAojcfPy6YRsZAJFXYNQQ&hl=en&sa=X&ved=2ahUKEwix9Jmns8ngAhWis1kKHQNaBBo4FBDoATAHegQIARAB#v

Frenez, Dennys; Jamison, Gregg; Law, Randall; Vidale, Massimo; Measdow, Richard. *Walking with the Unicorn, social organization and material culture in ancient south Asia.* Archaeopress Publishing, Oxford. 2018

Gadd, C. J. "Seals of Ancient Indian Style Found at Ur." *Proceedings of the British Academy* 18 (1932):191-210.

Giovino, Mariana. "The Assyrian Sacred Tree: A History of Interpretations", *Journal of the American Oriental Society*, Vol. 128, No. 4 (Oct. - Dec., 2008), pp.757-758 https://www.jstor.org/stable/25608460

Gosse, P.H. *Romance of Natural History*: https://archive.org/details/romanceofnatural00goss_13

Grotte de Rouffignac
http://www.grottederouffignac.fr/index.php/en/10-fr-fr/16-collectionneurs

Hafford, William B. "Mesopotamian City Life" *Expedition* Vol. 60, Issue 1, 2018 https://www.penn.museum/sites/expedition/mesopotamian-city-life/

Hall, M. D. *A Study of Sumerian Moon God Nanna/Suen.* Ph.D. thesis, University of Pennsylvania, 1985 http://repository.upenn.edu/dissertations/AAI8603645/
Peregrine, Peter, Ember, Melvin, editors.

Haleem, Asia. "The Cannon of Ancient Near Eastern Art. Catalogues of Evidence." http://www.layish.co.uk/catalogue_e_1_art_history.pdf

Indicopleustes, Cosmas. *Christian Topography*. Roger Pearse, Translator. http://www.tertullian.org/fathers/cosmas_11_book11.htm

Jastrow, Morris. *Aspects of Religious Belief and Practice in Babylonia and Assyria.* G.P. Putnam's Sons, New York. 1911.
https://archive.org/details/aspectsofreligio00jast/page/n207/mode/2up

Jastrow, Morris. *Handbooks on the history of religions volume II, The Religion of Babylonia and Assyria.* The Athenaeum Press, Boston. 1893.
https://www.gutenberg.org/files/20758/20758-h/20758-h.htm

Johnsgard, Paul and Karin. *A Natural History Dragons and Unicorns.* 1982, St. Martin's Press, New York

Kenoyer, Jonathan Mark. "Walking with the Unicorn". *Social Organization and Material Culture in Ancient South Asia*, http://www.archaeopress.com/public/download.asp?id=%7BD0F0019C-6D8C-4F68-861F-CA8F11E32CD8%7D

Kenoyer, Jonathan Mark. "Iconography of the Indus Unicorn: Origins and Legacy." *Connections and Complexity, New Approaches to the Archaeology of South Asia.* 2013

Kramer, Samuel Noah. *Sumerian Mythology.* Harper and Brothers, New York 1961

Kramer, Samuel Noah. *The Sumerians, their history, culture, and character.* University of Chicago Press, 1963

Lavers, Chris. *The Natural History of Unicorns.* 2009 Harper Collins Publishers, New York

Leibowitz, Rachel "Art History's 8 Greatest Unicorns from Met Tapestries to Damien Hirst's Taxidermy". *Artsy.* https://www.artsy.net/article/artsy-editoriAl-art-historys-8-greatest-unicorns-met-tapestries-damien-hirsts-taxidermy

Liebenberg, W.A. *A Historical Research of the Ten Tribes Scattered Into the Nations.* Hebraic Roots Teaching Institute Gauteng – South Africa 2016

Parpola, Asko, "Unicorn Bull and Victory Parade." *Walking with the Unicorn*, Archaeopress, Oxford. 2018 pages 433-442

Photius of Constantinople, *Bibliotheca.* http://www.tertullian.org/fathers/photius_03bibliotheca.htm

Place, Victor. *Ninive et l'Assyrie* (Tafeln) Paris, 1867 https://digitalcollections.nypl.org/items/510d47e2-f667-a3d9-e040-e00a18064a99/book?parent=f1a4e960-c6d3-012f-b5b0-58d385a7bc34#page/1/mode/2up

Pliny, *Natural History*, Book 8 Chapter 31. I used the translation found here: http://artflsrv02.uchicago.edu/cgi-bin/perseus/citequery3.pl?dbname=LatinSept18&getid=1&query=Plin.%20Nat.%208.31

Ray, Satyajit *The Unicorn Expedition.* E.P. Dutton New York, 1987

Rightmire, G. Phillip, "Middle and Later Pleistocene hominins in Africa and Southwest Asia" *Proceedings of the National Academy of Sciences of the United States of America* https://www.pnas.org/content/

pnas/106/38/16046.full.pdf

Rogers, John. *Origins of the ancient constellations*. British Astronomical Association, 1988. http://articles.adsabs.harvard.edu/cgi-bin/nph-iarticle_query?bibcode=1998JBAA..108....9R&db_key=AST&page_ind=0&plate_select=NO&data_type=GIF&type=SCREEN_GIF&classic=YES

Schvyreva, A.K. *On the importance of the representatives of the genus Elasmotherium (Rhinocerotidae, Mammalia) in the biochronology of the Pleistocene of Eastern Europe*. Elsevier. May 16, 2015.

Shepard, Odell. *The Lore of the Unicorn*. Harper Colophon Books, New York, 1956. A copy of the text can be found here: http://www.sacred-texts.com/etc/lou/index.htm

Shurpin, Yehuda. https://www.chabad.org/library/article_cdo/aid/4298548/jewish/What-Was-the-Mysterious-Tachash.htm

Smith, George; Sayce, Archibald Henry. *The Chaldean Account of Genesis*. https://www.gutenberg.org/files/60559/60559-h/60559-h.htm

Staff. "Jesus and the Unicorn: Easter and the Harrowing of Hell in Coptic Magic". Coptic Magical Papyri. 2019. http://www.coptic-magic.phil.uni-wuerzburg.de/index.php/2019/04/26/jesus-and-the-unicorn-easter-and-the-harrowing-of-hell-in-coptic-magic/

Swanson, Emily. "Harappan Civilization", *India and Southern Asia Chronology*. 2020 http://www.thenagain.info/WebChron/India/Harappa.html

Suckling, Nigel. *Unicorns*. AAPPL Artists' and Photographers' Press, 2007

Sharples, Tiffany. "A Brief History of the Unicorn" *Time*. 2008 http://content.time.com/time/health/article/0,8599,1814227,00.html

Sooke, Alastair. "Why We've Always Loved Unicorns", *Culture*. https://www.bbc.com/culture/article/20181214-why-weve-always-loved-unicorns Dec. 17, 2018

Spense, Lewis. *Myths and Legends of Babylonia and Assyria*. George Harrap & Company, London. 1920. https://archive.org/stream/mythslegendsofba00spenuoft/mythslegendsofba00spenuoft#page/230/mode/1up

Thompson, Gary. "Early Mesopotamian Constellations." https://web.archive.org/web/20150907050519/http://members.westnet.com.au/Gary-

David-Thompson/page11-4.html and https://web.archive.org/web/20121114124324/http://members.westnet.com.au/Gary-David-Thompson/page11-5.html

Throop, Pricilla. Translator. *Hildegard von Bingen's Physica: The Complete English Translation of Her Classic Work on Health and Healing*, Simon and Schuster, 1998

Vajracharya, Gautama. "Unicorns in Ancient India and Vedic Ritual". *Electronic Journal of Vedic Studies*, Volume 17, Issue 2. 2010 https://doi.org/10.11588/ejvs.2010.2.322

West, E. W. *Sacred Books of the East*, Oxford University Press, 1897. http://www.avesta.org/mp/bundahis.html#chapter19

West, E. W. *Sacred Books of the East*, Oxford University Press, 1897. http://avesta.org/yasna/yasna.htm#y35 (chapter 42 is at the end of this section)

Wright Thomas, M.A., F.S.A. *The History of Caricature and Grotesque in Literature and Art*, Chatto and Windus, Piccadilly. 1875. https://www.google.com/books/edition/A_History_of_Caricature_and_Grotesque_in/Pos741KQFtcC?hl=en&gbpv=1&printsec=frontcover

Wolkstein, Diane; Kramer, Samuel Noah. *Inanna, Queen of Heaven and Earth*. Harper and Row, New York. 1983

von Bunsen, Christian Karl Josias Freiherr; Birch, Samuel; Philo of Byblos. *Egypt's Place in Universal History*. University of Michigan, 1848 https://www.google.com/books/edition/_/JpBJAAAAMAAJ?hl=en&gbpv=0

Von Der Osten, Hans Henning. "The Ancient Seals from the Near East in the Metropolitan Museum: Old and Middle Persian Seals." *The Art Bulletin*, vol. 13, no. 2, 1931, pp. 221–241. JSTOR, www.jstor.org/stable/3050798. Accessed 18 June 2020.

Woolley, Leonard. *Ur*. Penguin Books LTD, New York, 1946

Zhegallo, V.; Kalandadze, N.; Shapovalov, A.; Bessudnova, Z.; Noskova, N.; Tesakova, E. (2005). "On the fossil rhinoceros Elasmotherium (including the collections of the Russian Academy of Sciences)" http://www.rhinoresourcecenter.com/pdf_files/142/1429150376.pdf. *Cranium*. 22 (1): 17–40.

https://allnurseryrhymes.com/the-lion-and-the-unicorn/

https://www.heraldryandcrests.com/pages/heraldic-symbolism-a-z

ABOUT THE AUTHOR

An information security executive by day, W. B. J. Williams' secret identity is that of an author. He also holds advanced degrees in anthropology and archeology, as well as being an avid historian, mystic, and poet. He is noted for his bad puns and willingness to argue from any perspective. He is endured by his beloved wife and two daughters, and lives in Sharon Massachusetts. When he is not at home or at his computer, he can often be found haunting the various used bookstores of Boston. His publishing credits include: *The Garden at the Roof of the World*, with Dragonwell Publishing, "The Info-Coup" with *Abyss and Apex*, *Information Security for Service Oriented Architecture* with CRC Press, and *The Reality, Mythology, and Fantasies of Unicorns* with Dragonwell Publishing. *How to Create an Information Security Program from Scratch* is currently in production with CRC Press and is planned for September 2021. He is a frequent author panelist at ReaderCon and Arisia, and has been a panelist at Boskone.

Read more about the magic of unicorns in:

THE GARDEN
AT THE ROOF OF THE WORLD

W. B. J. WILLIAMS

Dragonwell Publishing

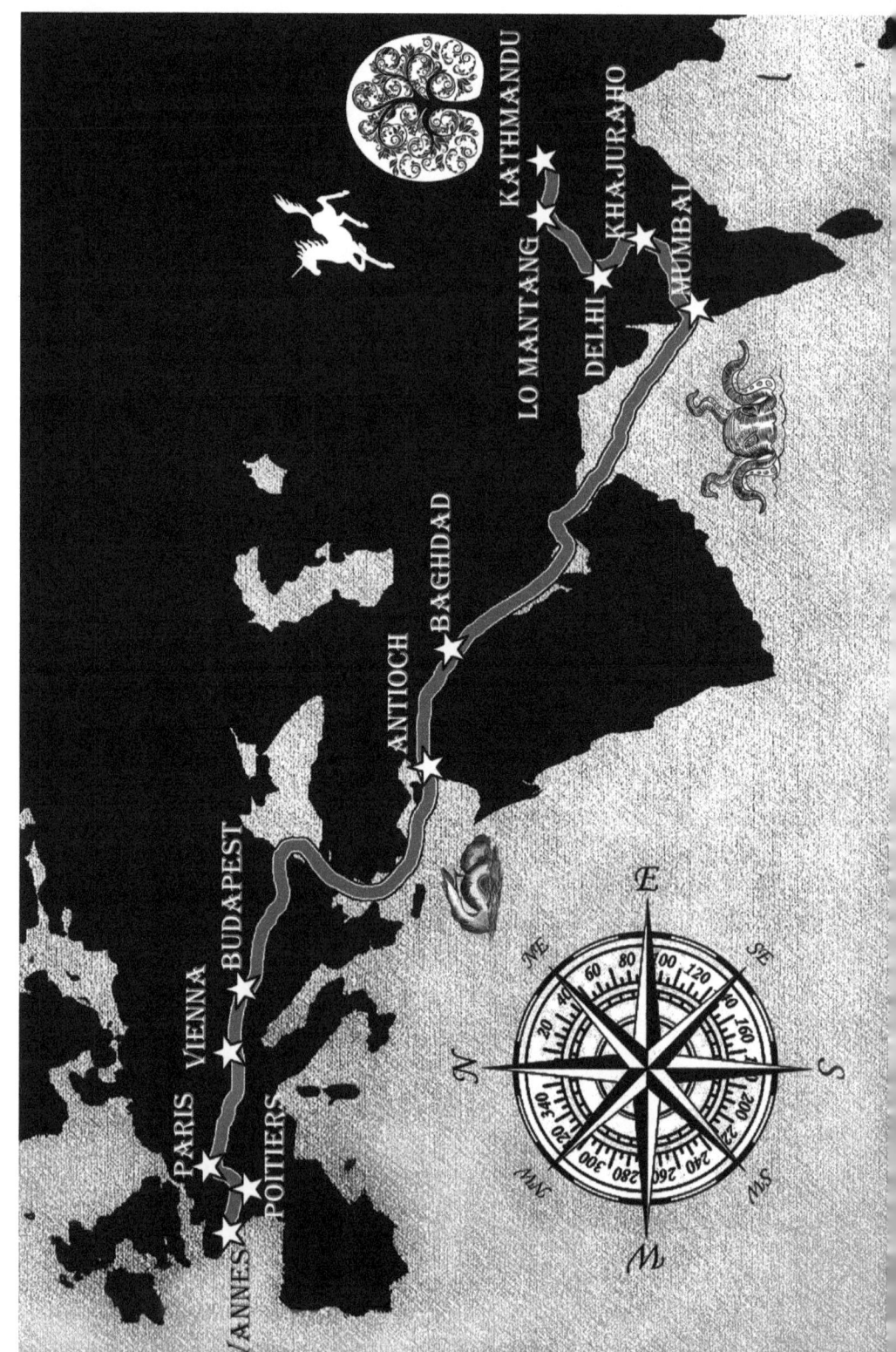

A LETTER

Namaste, Sri[1] Thomas of Aquinas, my most esteemed friend! I have reached the twilight of my years and at long last have the leisure to write to you in full about the women who accompanied the unicorn. Their story is a rich one, and I am glad to have taken the final steps of their journey with them.

After the bird brought your note, I went to wait for the maidens and the unicorn with two men of my village. Great was my joy when I saw them climb up the stone stairs of the mountain passes, and they accepted me as their guide. During the long nights of our journey to the Garden, and over the course of many weeks, I learned the fullness of their adventures. The Buddha has blest me with an excellent memory, so I hope to faithfully relate to you their stories in their own words.

It is the women who told most of the tale. The men would say little of their deeds. They once told me that only the women were called to serve the unicorns in their need, and the men followed because of their love of the women. I realized the truth of this myself when the Yeti came to destroy us. I count myself fortunate to have survived, if for no other reason than to convey to you their story.

I wish you well in your studies, my old friend, and look forward to renewing our correspondence of old.

Prince Jigme of Lo Mantang

---

[1]Translator's note: Namaste is Sanskrit for "I bow to the god within you" and is often used to recognize a common divinity within the other person. There is no English cognate, and it is commonly not translated. Sri is a title which means "Lord".

GWENAELLA

Gwenaella's call to serve the unicorns came from the First Woman herself.

Late and under the cover of darkness, she scrambled over the convent's wall, clutching the manuscript her dear love had given her in their tryst under the fig trees. Her heart raced at the memory of his embrace, his promise of marriage, and his kiss.

Gwen clutched the manuscript to her bosom as she pulled herself up the rose-covered trellis. Years of use by other students had provided a thorn-free path that she'd followed for her weekly trysts with Guillaume. She pushed herself up another rung and slid the manuscript onto the top of the wall, then pulled herself up beside it. She forced herself to lay still, to quiet her breathing. Below, she could hear the soft crunch of footsteps on the path along the wall. One of the nuns must be patrolling for students like her, hiding to avoid punishment for leaving the convent. Guillaume's gift would doom her to a dual punishment—not only for sneaking out, but also for possessing a romance. She smiled. Guillaume had written this romance specifically for her. Reading this would be worth any penance.

Finally only the sounds of crickets and tree frogs met her ears. She grabbed the manuscript and crawled along the top of the wall to where it met the roof of the dormitory that she shared with the daughters of wealthy merchants. Like her, they'd been sent here to learn how to be good wives to even wealthier merchants. Guillaume had promised to spare her that fate.

She grabbed hold of the gargoyle and swung herself down to the ledge just beneath the window, left open to the summer's cool evening air. She stepped through the window onto the soft rushes that the girls lay on the floor each evening to cover the hot stone and give warning of the nun's heavy tread. She moved as cautiously as possible but Rimoete sat up as she passed her bed, her dark tresses spilling out of her nightcap.

"Gwenaella," she whispered, "How did your tryst go?"

Gwen leaned over and whispered in her ear. "Guillaume is off to

Paris to seek his father's blessing for a betrothal."

Rimoete kissed her on the cheek. "God bless! You are a fortunate maid! What is this you hold?"

Gwen hugged the manuscript close to her bosom. "Guillaume wrote a romance for me."

"Oh, you are lucky in your love. I'm quite jealous, you know. Now go, Sister Switch is on the prowl."

Gwen kissed her for the fair warning. She slipped the manuscript under her pillow, undressed, and slid under the coverings. Her evening prayers were of joyous gratitude and pleas for Guillaume's father's blessing.

Gwen waited three hours before daring to light a grease candle and read Guillaume's romance. She sat on the edge of her bed, tracing each word with her finger as she silently mouthed them. Words he'd written with her in mind; a gift of undying love.

A soft shuffle on the rushes broke her rapture. One of the nuns. The smell of the burning grease must have given her away again. She quickly put away the manuscript, replacing it with another, left open for just this purpose. It was a brilliantly illuminated Psalter; with a magnificent drawing opposite each page to show some of the divine truth found in the sacred text. Gwen bent over it, her copper tresses mingling with the gilt of the illustration.

Gwen let the nun stand over her a moment before glancing up from the Psalter she pretended to read. She recognized the nun's scowl-lined face at once and tried not to wince as she said, "Sister Clair, what brings you to my side at this hour?"

The nun clicked her tongue, pulling the book off Gwen's pillow. "What are you reading, child? If this is another romance, your penance will be stiff."

Gwen remained silent, waiting for the text to answer the lie. Her rump still hurt from the last penance Sister Clair had administered.

"Why, Gwenaella! I'm proud of you. Psalm 8 is one of my favorites. '*Quid est homo quod memor es eius aut filius hominis quoniam visitas eum.*'[1] Wonderful, isn't it? Still, you should be resting." The nun closed the Psalter and blew out Gwen's candle. "I'm heartened to observe that my loving ministrations and prayers said in your benefit are having an effect. May the Good Lord bless you, my daughter."

---

[1]Translator's note: Sister Clair quotes from the Vulgate, Psalm 8 verse 5: For you have made him a little lower than the angels, and have crowned him with glory and honor.

GWENAELLA

As Sister Clair shuffled away, beads clicking in rhythm to her stride, Gwen smiled and pushed the manuscript she had actually been reading deeper under her pillow. Loving ministrations indeed. Gwen hugged the pillow, hoping Tadig[2] would consent to their marriage. While Guillaume was not the merchant he'd hoped for his daughter, perhaps being a scholar's wife would be permitted. She rose up onto her knees and prayed that she'd be permitted to marry for love.

The remnants of the night's rain glistened in the cold light of dawn as it dripped off the adjoining roof and slid down the spiral pillars of the cloister. Gwenaella hurried alongside Rimoete through the herb garden. They wore the shapeless white gowns of the convent students, though Rimoete had already pulled on the wimple Gwen had been struggling with.

Rimoete said, "I don't understand. How can it be that Guillaume wrote that the door to Pleasure's garden is opened by Idleness?"

Gwen, who was trying hard to straighten the wimple over her loose curls, said, "The girl's name was Idleness. What I don't understand is why there was an image of poverty alongside images of avarice and envy."

"Why that's silly," said Rimoete. "They're all images of things you don't want, things that keep you from pleasure. What a shame that Sister Clair should interrupt you. Has Guillaume already returned to Paris?"

Gwen's foot caught on a loose flagstone, and she tumbled to the ground. Annoyed with herself, she accepted Rimoete's offered hand and pulled herself to her feet. They both brushed the leaves and dirt from her gown.

As Gwen bent down to retrieve her wimple from the damp ground, she heard Sister Clair say, "Our Lord is also a stumbling block for the sinful, Gwenaella."

She looked up and saw the nun enter the cloister from the direction they were heading, face hidden in the bright light of dawn beyond her. "I don't know if finishing your dressing while you rush to matins is a sin, Sister," said Gwen defiantly.

"Sloth, my child, is a sin and a grave one at that. Well, I must say I'm going to miss giving you the whipping that such a remark merits. You've been sent for."

---

[2]Translator's note: Tadig is Breton for Daddy.

"Sent for, Sister?" Gwen felt the chills as she detected pity in the nun's tone. It could only be bad news. It was much too fast for Guillaume to have reached Tadig, or the word of an accepted approval of a marriage to reach her.

"Yes, follow me."

Rimoete embraced Gwen. "I'll keep you in my prayers."

"Thank you," Gwen whispered. She straightened her gown and followed the nun. Hurried footsteps echoed behind and someone gently pressed the wimple into her hand. She dared not turn to thank her friend, whose hand she briefly squeezed in gratitude.

The nun led her to the stone chapel where the priest would come once a day to say Mass. This was the only place where a man was permitted in the convent. Gwen's father might have found her a husband, some fat, rich, probably old merchant who would take her with her education still incomplete. Ah, Guillaume! So much for prayers answered.

The nun pulled open the brown wooden door carved with the words *"Petite, et dabitur vobis: quærite, et invenietis: pulsate, et aperietur vobis."*[3] She beckoned Gwen to enter.

Gwen hesitated; the dark of the chamber was foreboding. It took her a moment to adjust to the dim lighting afforded by the stained glass windows and see a man rising from where he knelt before the crucifix.

"Gwen, I'd had never known you, you've grown so."

"Uncle Boduuan!" She recognized the voice, his face was still in shadow. "I was told I've been sent for, but no one told me who, nor why."

"It's your brother. He's really sick."

"Sam's ill?" Gwen felt faint. "How so?"

"He's wasting away; he has no strength, and can barely keep down broth. I doubt he'll last a fortnight."

"Sancta Maria!" Blood rushed to Gwen's head like pounding surf.

She felt a soft hand upon her back and turned to see a familiar wrinkled face marked by years of scowls. The Mother Superior.

"Gwenaella, I heard about the summons and came as quickly as I could. While perhaps not all the Sisters agree with me, I will miss you, my child. In my heart, I had always hoped you would take up orders and join us."

Gwen bowed her head. "Mother, I must do my father's will. I will miss you as well." She felt a pang of guilt that despite the grave

---

[3]Translator's note: Matthew 7: Ask, and it shall be given you; seek, and you shall find; knock and it shall be opened to you.

situation she was secretly glad she was leaving.

"Yes, your father will need you to bring a son-in-law into his house, to take over with the boat and tend him in his old age. May you find joy in your husband." There was genuine pity in her old brown eyes.

"Thank you, Mother. Uncle, I will need just a moment to gather my things." *Pulsate, et aperietur vobis* indeed. The nun was right about one thing: the door from this joyless chamber led not to Heaven and love's promise fulfilled, but to bondage of a loveless marriage.

Through the cloister with flowers that no longer had any color to her, Gwen rushed to outrun her tears. Sam was ill. That lone fact hammered at her, making her grief at her broken marital hopes into a selfish ache. Whatever had laid her strong brother low?

Gwen returned to her room. Light streaming through the cracks in the shutters made the white plaster walls seem gray and shoddy. She walked over to the window and threw it open. A breeze caught her hair and blew the tears out of the corners of her eyes so they ran freely down her cheeks. There must be a way to open the door to health, to keep Sam from the grave. Perhaps some of the herb lore that Sister Clair had taught might revive him. If she could but restore him to health, surely Tadig would let her marry Guillaume.

She went to her pallet where her small chest of unvarnished wood stood, a contrast to the varnished and carved chests of the girls she had spent the last three years of her life with. They had learnt much from each other, these daughters of wealth and she, a fisherman's waif. She never understood how was it that Tadig had found the means to send her to the convent school, and always knew the price she'd have to pay would be a marriage to some wealthy merchant. She'd been content with this until she met Guillaume. Now life without him seemed a cruel jest.

She sighed and opened her chest. Sam was dying. The rest was not important.

Under her rags and shift, she found a blue woolen bliault[4] with a red velvet mantle and a white lace coif. She gently laid these on her pallet, and pulled off her gown as quickly as she could, tossing it to the corner of the room and replacing it with the clothes she had unpacked. Then she reached under her pillow and grabbed Guillaume's manuscript. Gwen's finger traced the handwritten title: *le Roman de la Rose*.[5] Remembering last night, when Guillaume had given his

---

[4]Translator's note: a garment commonly worn during the 12th century, it would have been out of fashion by the time Gwenaella wore it in the mid 13th.

[5]Translator's note: The Romance of the Rose. Guillaume is the author of the first part.

writing to her and professed his undying love, she hugged it as if holding Guillaume and his promise. After a moment she placed it in her trunk, wiped away the tears and took a deep breath. She knelt and brought her hands together. "Dearest Mary, ever a friend to women, let there be a way to restore Sam." She crossed herself and rose.

She placed the chest over her shoulder the way she often saw her father do. The weight of it made her stoop as she walked. She was glad when her uncle met her at the bottom of the stairs and took the chest from her. Rubbing the tears from the corners of her eyes, she followed him down the cut stone halls of the convent.

Sister Bodhicca, a young nun Gwen liked very much, waited for them at the wrought iron gate. Uncle Boduuan put down the chest while Gwen embraced the nun.

"I have a small present for you, Gwenaella," Bodhicca said, handing her the same Psalter she'd been pretending to read. "Sister Clair told me how you stay up at night reading it, and I thought that if you loved the psalms so much, you should have a Psalter of your own."

Gwen blushed and hugged Sister Bodhicca tightly, now shamed by her duplicity. Trying to sound sincere, she said, "This is a lovely gift, but it must have cost you a fortune. It should stay here, in the convent, where it may delight all your students."

"No, please take it. I insist."

Gwen took the Psalter and embraced the nun again. Its songs of loss would be a comfort.

Sister Bodhicca unhitched the lever to unlock the gate, and pulled it open with a screech. Gwen and her uncle each carried their burdens into the street. There waited a pony cart, a novice holding the tether. Uncle Boduuan put the trunk into the cart, then lifted Gwen into the seat. He took the tether from the novice and led the pony into the crowded streets.

The sun shone bright in their eyes as Gwen and her uncle made their way through Vannes. Neither knew the streets well, so they went slowly, meandering through the crowds of carts, horses and men.

"Way! Make way!" a man shouted from behind them, followed by the thunder of hooves. Boduuan guided his pony cart to the side of the street, along with many in the throng. Gwen watched as a knight galloped down the street. Dust covered his device; blood stained his surcoat.

A loud scream echoed through the crowd in his wake. Gwen jumped off the cart and pushed through the throng to the fallen old woman. She lay in the dust, her face a mess of blood from a large cut on her forehead. Gwen pulled her handkerchief from her sleeve and wiped the blood, trying to keep it away from the woman's clear gray-green eyes.

"Mother, pray tell, what happened?"

"A stone kicked up by the horse hit me," the hurt woman moaned.

Gwen slipped her arms under the woman and tried to lift her. Strange, the old woman smelled of a fresh sea breeze. Gwen shook off her confusion. What did it matter if the old woman did not smell of stale sweat and blood, what did it matter if the woman's green eyes were not clouded with age? She couldn't lift her alone. "Uncle Boduuan, help me carry her back to the convent. She needs care."

He scowled. "Gwen, that stone must be the Good Lord's warning to the witch, cast from the destrier's hooves. Leave her."

"Uncle, how can you speak ill of this poor woman?"

"Don't you notice, no one else is coming to her aid? Surely she is a witch. Now, let's go, your brother needs you."

"If you don't help me carry her to the convent, I'll carry her myself!"

Her uncle looked into her face and turned away, his cheeks red. He grunted as he shifted the old woman's weight, lifting her gently into the cart. Gwen sat next to her, holding her hand as her uncle pulled them back the way they'd come.

"Child," whispered the old woman, "Seek a unicorn under the eaves of Brocéliande."

Gwen's heart skipped a beat. No mother of children would tell her to enter that wood. Perhaps her uncle was right and this woman was a witch. Besides, seeking unicorns was a quest for ladies, not the likes of her. "Why should I risk such a thing? What would a unicorn want with me, I'm no lady."

"Hush child, you'll know why soon enough. Go, seek a unicorn."

Gwen had begun to regret helping this woman, she must be a witch, but when they got to the gate, she hopped out of the cart and pulled the bell chain three times. Witch or not, the old woman was hurt.

Sister Bodhicca was soon opening the gate. "Bring her in! I'll get Sister Clair."

Uncle Boduuan laid the old woman down on the bench, backed away and crossed himself. The woman smiled at Gwen. "You've got a good heart. Thank you, dear."

Once Sister Bodhicca returned with Sister Clair, Uncle Boduuan and Gwen left the convent. Gwen silently pondered the old woman's words as they traveled.

In the three days it took them to travel from the Convent of St. Armel in Vannes to the village of Redon where her family lived, Gwen had plenty of time to think on ways to restore Sam to health. There were various herbs whose restorative powers she would try. If rosemary didn't work, perhaps ginger would. If he was in tremendous pain, some clove would help.

As the sun reached its zenith on that third day, they crested a hill and saw two rivers gleaming in the sun with Redon at the fork. Gwen, who had been leading the pony as her uncle rested in the cart, paused for a moment to look upon a place she had not seen in three years. From this distance, the stink of the salt houses pungent with the odor of fish could not mar the beauty of the peaceful town of thatched-roof cottages and the sun-bright river that ran through it. Beyond it loomed the dark shadow of the Brocéliande Forest. Gwen shivered. No way she was entering that wood—certainly not on some witch's urging. Tadig's home stood close to the forest, and she'd grown to womanhood in terror of its dark secrets and the enchantress that lived there.

She clicked her tongue and led the pony down the hill. Soon she switched with her uncle and sat on the cart, while he guided the pony through the village streets. The packed mud walls and thatched roofs brought a bitter sort of joy. She'd missed them so. She had often longed to flee the stone of the cloister for straw-swept dirt floors and the smell of fish stew. And now, instead of the joy she'd dreamed of upon her homecoming, she dreaded it. Did Sam still live?

Her parents' home seemed to have an aura of doom about it. The garden was overgrown with weeds, and the roof's thatching bare in more than one place. The shade from the forest made the walls seem gray and forlorn.

Uncle Boduuan brought the cart to a halt. Gwen hopped out, lifting the chest to her shoulder, and her uncle opened the door for her. "Tell your father that I will drop by in a few days to help out with repairing the roof. I've been away too long from your aunt and I want to look in on her, and then I'll need to work the boat before I have enough to spare another journey."

Gwen kissed him on his rough cheek. "Thank you so much, Uncle. I'll let him know."

She stepped inside to find the hearth cold, only embers left of the coals that should have had the evening stew simmering over it.

GWENAELLA

A smell puzzled her, something out of place. *Incense.* Fearing the worst, she put down her chest and opened the door to the extension Sam had built onto the house when he'd come of age, a room of his own.

www.ingramcontent.com/pod-product-compliance
Lightning Source LLC
Chambersburg PA
CBHW041325110526

44592CB00021B/2821